Adult Winter Bible Study

Hosea: God's Redeeming Love

John Traylor

Convention Press • Nashville, Tennessee

Contents

5403-94

Dewey Decimal Classification Number: 224.6
Subject Heading: BIBLE. O.T. HOSEA
Printed in the United States of America.

This book is the text for a course in the subject area Bible Study of the Church Study Course.

Target group: This book is designed for adults and is part of the Church Study Course offerings. The 1963 statement of *The Baptist Faith and Message* is the doctrinal guideline for the writer and editor.

A Word to Begin

Hosea's experiences and messages, clearly portrayed in the fourteen chapters of his book, lead the reader to a spiritual awareness of the ruin caused by sin, the inevitability of divine judgment on sin, and the loyal love of God for the sinful. No other book in the Old Testament, I believe, more graphically sets forth these realities.

Perhaps the dominant theme discovered in the pages of Hosea is the love of God—a love so deep and so steadfast that continued immorality by God's people, though despised, is forgiven. Who can read, unmoved, the compassionate appeal of God to His wayward own: "How can I give you up, O Ephraim? My heart is turned over within Me, All my compassions are kindled?" (11:8) The story of Hosea's love for and marriage to Gomer, overcoming at last all the heartbreaks of her sinful life, is a story worth hearing again and again. God, too, reaches to love and rejoices in the relationship.

The writer is Dr. John Traylor. Dr. Traylor received a Doctor of Theology Degree in Hebrew and Old Testament interpretation from the New Orleans Baptist Theological Seminary, New Orleans, Louisiana. He presently serves as pastor to the First Baptist Church, Monroe, Louisiana, and is president of the Executive Board, Louisiana Baptist Convention. He has many published works.

The textbook is written for either personal or group study. The Lessons For Life at each chapter's conclusion should help in applying Hosea's words to life today. The *Expository Notes* and the *Resource Kit for Hosea: God's Redeeming Love* will help the teacher to direct and guide the study.

A Church Study Course Credit request is on page 128. On completing this book, the reader should fill out Form 725 and mail to the indicated address.

Ben Garner, editor

1

HOSEA'S CALL AND MARRIAGE

Hosea 1:1—2:1

My wife, Betty Colvin Traylor, is the greater part of my glory. I have to give the Lord credit for my having her as a beloved helpmate.

Betty almost married another man. In fact, everyone assumed that she and her childhood sweetheart would marry. God intended her for me and has given us a wonderful marriage with two wonderful daughters, both of whom now are married and each has a son.

The secret of our love is the Lord Jesus Christ. Indeed, making Him Lord of our lives is the reason that we love each another with all of our hearts. The Lord gave us our home of permanence and love, and we praise Him.

Our relationship goes back to our courting days at Louisiana Tech where we met, fell in love, and married. Even while we whispered "sweet somethings" to each other under the stars, we by God's grace vowed to God and to each other to make Christ the Lord of our home.

We struggled during the first months of our marriage. One reason was the normal problems of newlyweds learning to live together. Another reason was that during the first months of our marriage, I lived under the shadow of Betty's childhood sweetheart. Still, Betty and I kept pressing upward, ever closer to God and thus to one another. I'm not sure exactly when it happened, but one day we both realized that we belong totally and lovingly to God and to each other.

Hosea is the prophet of God's redeeming love. Like me, he learned of God's love through marriage. His experience broke his heart at first. His wife did not join him in pressing upward, ever closer to God. Rather, she turned from God and then from Hosea. Hosea remained faithful to her through God's steadfast love. In the end, Hosea found love from God powerful enough to redeem even his wayward wife.

General Introduction

The Book of Hosea is the first of the prophetic books in the section of the Bible spoken of as the Minor Prophets. These twelve books begin with Hosea and continue through Malachi. These books are not "minor" because their message is less significant. Rather, they are called "minor" because of their length. These books are short compared with Isaiah, Jeremiah, and Ezekiel—the Major Prophets.

Hosea was the second of God's spokesmen known as the eighth-century prophets. In order of their appearance, these prophets were Amos, Hosea, Isaiah, and Micah. (See Amos 1:1; Hos. 1:1; Isa. 1:1; 6:1; and Mic. 1:1.) Hosea and his contemporary Amos spoke to the Northern Kingdom, composed of the ten northern tribes and usually called Israel. Isaiah and Micah prophesied primarily to the Southern Kingdom, composed of Judah, Benjamin, and other tribes loyal to the house of David. The Southern Kingdom is usually called Judah. (See 1 Kings 11:30-32; 12:21.)

Since Hosea and Amos both spoke to the Northern Kingdom at about the same time in history, the messages of the two prophets have much in common. Each prophet, however, had some distinctive emphases. Like Hosea, Amos spoke of the future restoration of the people of Israel as a united kingdom under the house of David (Amos 9:11-15). Amos' main emphasis was upon God's judgment that would destroy the northern tribes as a separate nation. Hosea, like Amos, prophesied the destruction of the Northern Kingdom. However, Hosea magnified God's redeeming love that would lead ultimately to the salvation of a united Israel under the house of David (Hos. 1:11; 3:5).

Hosea has 2 main divisions: Hosea's marriage (1-3) and message (4-14). Four themes occur in the book: God's love, sin, judgment, and hope. These themes interweave throughout the book, but each is given special emphasis in certain parts of Hosea's prophecy. Hosea 1:1—3:5 emphasizes God's faithful love in spite of the people's unfaithfulness to Him. Hosea 4:1—7:16 shows God's indictment of the sins of unfaithful Israel. Hosea 8:1—10:15 stresses the sure judgment that awaited Israel because of their stubborn refusal to repent. Hosea 11:1—14:9 presents the hope that God's healing love will eventually lead some to repentance and renewal.

These four themes speak powerfully to us and our generation. Hosea identifies our basic sin as unfaithfulness to God. God's Word indicts us for our many sins and warns of sure judgment against persistent sin. Above all, God's Word through Hosea extends the invitation to life and hope based on God's great love.

Summary of Hosea 1:1—2:1

The prophetic ministry of Hosea, through whom God revealed His redeeming love, began with God's command for Hosea to take for himself "a wife of harlotry, and have children of harlotry" (1:2). Through Hosea's heartbreak in relation to his wife's unfaithfulness, God enabled Hosea to understand God's heartbreak over Israel's unfaithfulness to Him.

Three children were born to Hosea and his wife Gomer. Only the first was clearly stated to be Hosea's child (1:3,6,8). In obedience to God's command, Hosea pictured through the naming of the children the judgment God would bring upon faithless Israel (1:4-9). However, God and Hosea used these same names to picture the new beginning and ultimate redemption God would bring to the people of Israel following His judgment of them (1:10—2:1).

God's Word Through Hosea (1:1)

The Book of Hosea is our only source of personal information concerning Hosea, and it is quite limited except in relation to Hosea's marriage to Gomer (1:2-9; 3:1-3). For example, the name *Hosea* occurs only three times in the entire book (1:1,2). We know nothing about *Beeri* except that he was Hosea's father. We do understand from the book that Hosea was a native of and God's spokesman to the Northern Kingdom. As such, Hosea is in contrast with Amos, who spoke to Israel but lived in Judah (Amos 1:1). The familiarity of the name *Hosea* (Hoshea) to the Ephraimites suggests that Hosea was of the tribe of Ephraim, which was the predominant tribe of Israel. (See Num. 13:8; 1 Chron. 27:20; Hos. 5:1-15.)

Amos was a shepherd (Amos 7:14), but what was Hosea? We do not know. Some suppose Hosea was a priest because of his knowledge of that group (4:6-8; 5:1; 6:9). Others think Hosea was a farmer since he used numerous analogies from agricultural life (4:16; 10:12-13). Still others speculate that Hosea was a baker because of his analogy about the fiery oven (7:4-8). What we do know is that Hosea knew Israel, the people to whom he spoke, and the Lord God for whom he spoke.

The name *Hosea* (Hoshea) means "deliverance, rescue, salvation, safety." As such, the name is closely akin to that of Joshua ("the Lord saves," Num. 13:16) and that of Jesus who saves His people from their sin (Matt. 1:21). The name may point to the saved remnant that would dwell in safety forever under the house of David.

Verse 1 describes the book as "The word of the Lord which came to Hosea." God caused Hosea to see and to speak His word in an actual time and place. That word is binding upon every generation. The Book of Hosea is God's Word today. When we read it, believe it, and follow it, we experience the same steadfast and righteous love of God by which Hosea reclaimed and redeemed Gomer and God reclaimed and redeemed Israel.

Verse 1 identifies the time of Hosea's ministry by listing four kings of Judah and one king of Israel. The combined reigns of Uzziah, Jotham, Ahaz, and Hezekiah total approximately 113 years (see 2 Kings 15:2; 15:33; 16:2; 18:2). However, if you figure Hosea's ministry from the last days of Uzziah's reign to the sixth year of Hezekiah when the Northern Kingdom fell (2 Kings 18:10), you get a total of approximately 40 years (762-722 B.C.). The listing of these four kings shows that Hosea's ministry paralleled that of Isaiah (Isa. 1:1; 6:1).

Reference to Jeroboam, king of Israel, provides insights into the conditions in the Northern Kingdom when Hosea prophesied. This Jeroboam is identified as the son of Joash to distinguish him from Jeroboam the son of Nebat who was the Northern Kingdom's first king (1 Kings 11:26-40; 12:2).

Keep in mind four significant facts concerning Jeroboam the son of Joash, whom we usually call Jeroboam II. First, his reign testifies to God's faithfulness. Jeroboam reigned on the throne of Israel in fulfillment of God's promise to Jehu. God had rewarded Jehu for carrying out His command to cut off the house of Ahab (2 Kings 10:29-31,35).

Second, the reign of Jeroboam II testifies to God's compassion. During Jeroboam II's reign the Northern Kingdom enjoyed unprecedented peace, prosperity, and political expansion (2 Kings 14:25). However, these did not come because of Jeroboam's prowess, but because God chose him to answer Jeroboam's grandfather's prayer for relief to oppressed Israel from Syria (2 Kings 13:4-5; 14:25-27).

Third, Jeroboam's reign testifies to the terrible wickedness of the Northern Kingdom in the days that Hosea spoke for God. Their main sin was calf worship, which Jeroboam the son of Nebat established as the state religion. Every king after him, including Jeroboam the son of Joash, followed this idolatry. (For example, see 1 Kings 12:25-33; 15:26,34).

The two calves that Jeroboam the son of Nebat made and set up in Dan and Bethel were closely akin to the golden calf made by Aaron (Ex. 32:24). The calves (young bulls) were symbols of strength and virility. They were part of the fertility religion that demoralized Canaan as well as Egypt. Its devotees practiced prostitution in the name of religion to encourage their so-called gods (Baals) to mate in the heavens to produce fertility among crops, animals, and people on earth. The fertility cults spawned all sorts of sexual abuses including incest, adultery, child sacrifice, homosexuality, and bestiality for which God drove the Canaanites out of the land from before the face of Israel (see Lev. 18).

The worst part of the sin of Jeroboam the son of Nebat was his identifying the golden calves with the Lord God of Israel who brought them up from the land of Egypt (see 1 Kings 12:28). This corrupted true religion and spawned sexual sins by giving to the fertility cults the sanction of the Lord God of Israel. People tend toward sexual abuses by the corruption of their own nature. When people glorify sexual sins in the name of God, the sexual sins reproduce and spread to many others. Most likely Gomer was in some fashion a victim of fertility religion.

The fourth fact about Jeroboam II's reign was Assyria's emergence once again as the dominant power in the Middle East. With the death of Jeroboam II, the Northern Kingdom disintegrated rapidly. Zechariah, Jeroboam's son, reigned in his stead but was assassinated after six months on the throne (2 Kings 15:8-10). Five kings followed in rapid, turbulent succession (2 Kings 15:13-14; 17:1). By 722 B.C., the ninth year of Hoshea's reign as king of Israel and the sixth year of Hezekiah's reign as king of Judah, Assyria swept away forever the Northern Kingdom as a separate nation. (See 2 Kings 18:9-12.)

God's Word Through Hosea's Marriage (1:2)

Hosea's prophetic ministry began with the heart-piercing experience of having a wife who was a harlot. God in His gracious providence used the tragic experience of Hosea's broken home to open up Hosea's heart to God's word. God also used Hosea's marriage to illustrate His love for and ultimate redemption of harlot Israel.

God's word to Hosea in verse 2 has been the subject of much discussion. The wording, "Go, take to yourself a wife of harlotry," seems to imply that God told Hosea to marry a harlot. The discussion focuses on whether she was a harlot when Hosea married her or became one later.

One interpretation of "a wife of harlotry" is that although Gomer was probably chaste at the time of her marriage to Hosea, she soon gave way to her deeply rooted inclination toward harlotry. In turning from Hosea to other lovers, she depicted Israel turning to other gods after an initial stage of faithfulness to God (9:10; Jer. 2:2).

Others interpret "a wife of harlotry" to mean that Gomer at the time of their marriage was either a common prostitute, a temple prostitute, or a young woman who had sacrificed her virginity with priests at the altar of Baal to ensure her fertility in marriage. Advocates of this view claim that this is the most natural way to understand "Go, take to yourself a wife of harlotry."

Personally I prefer the first interpretation. The Mosaic law forbade a priest from marrying a harlot (Lev. 21:7). Would God have commanded a prophet to do what was forbidden to a priest?

Hosea was also told to "Have children of harlotry" (v. 2). These were children born to Gomer after her marriage to Hosea. *Have children of harlotry* may mean only that Hosea's children would take on the image of harlotry in having a harlot for their mother. However, it may mean that the children would inherit their mother's tendency toward harlotry and may even imply offspring of an adulterous union. Significantly, only the first child is said definitely to have been fathered by Hosea (v. 3). The omission of *him* in relation to the other two children (vv. 6,8) leaves open the possibility that these children were by someone other than Hosea.

Go, take does not suggest that God forced Hosea to marry Gomer, but leaves room for the normal process of courtship and marriage. What Hosea understood was that God would use Hosea's marriage to communicate the word of God, just as He often did in instructions to other prophets. (See Isa. 8:1; Jer. 27:1-2.) Hosea's marriage was to picture how Israel spiritually committed "flagrant harlotry" in turning from the Lord to serve other gods, especially Baal.

God's Word Through Hosea's Children (1:3-9)

What's in a name? Samuel Traylor Mann is the name of our young grandson. Our daughter Angela and son-in-law Kenny gave him that name to express their aspirations that their son be God's servant. *Samuel* comes from Samuel in the Bible. It also goes back to my grandfather, Samuel Scofield Bogan, who was a Methodist preacher. *Traylor* is after me. *Mann* is, of course, Kenny's family name. When my 84-year-old mother first saw Samuel Traylor and heard his name, she (who can see no wrong in the biblical Samuel, her father, or me) exclaimed: "Son, you have a lot to live up to."

Names are sometimes significant. Certainly, that was the

case with Hosea, his wife Gomer, and their three children. How would you like for your name to be Gomer, Jezreel, Lo-ruhamah, or Lo-ammi?

In obedience to God's command, Hosea took for his wife "Gomer the daughter of Diblaim" (1:3). *Diblaim* probably was the name of Gomer's father, but it may denote her hometown. *Gomer* is from a root meaning "to complete." In keeping with the double meaning of the names of the children born to Gomer, the name *Gomer* could point first to the completeness of her corruption and then to the perfection of her salvation through God's redeeming love. However, neither God nor Hosea states the significance of her name.

The children's names certainly became vehicles of revelation. God first used their names to point to the judgment that He would bring upon Israel for her sin (vv. 3-9). Then God and Hosea used the children's names to point to the redemption that God would bring to Israel through His steadfast and righteous love (vv. 10-11).

God commanded Hosea to name the first son *Jezreel* to declare the judgment that God would bring shortly on the house of Jehu and on the house of Israel (vv. 4-5). "The kingdom of the house of Israel" means the Northern Kingdom as a separate nation. God anointed and commissioned Jehu to destroy Ahab's house and to purge Baalism from Israel, previously introduced by Ahab and Jezebel (2 Kings 9:1-10). God rewarded Jehu for obedience to His command by promising that Jehu's descendants for four generations would reign over Israel (2 Kings 10:30). The sin for which God would shortly cut off Jehu's house was apparently twofold. First, Jehu used ruthless methods and had impure motives in exterminating the house of Ahab. Second, Jehu and his sons continued the calf worship established by Jeroboam the son of Nebat.

Jezreel was the fertile valley where Jezebel spilled Naboth's blood and Jehu spilled the blood of Ahab's house (1 Kings 21; 2 Kings 9—10). Its fruitfulness symbolized God's blessings upon the land. Now God would scatter the people in judgment by cutting off the house of Jehu and by destroying the Northern Kingdom as a separate nation.

In the day of God's destroying the Northern Kingdom, He

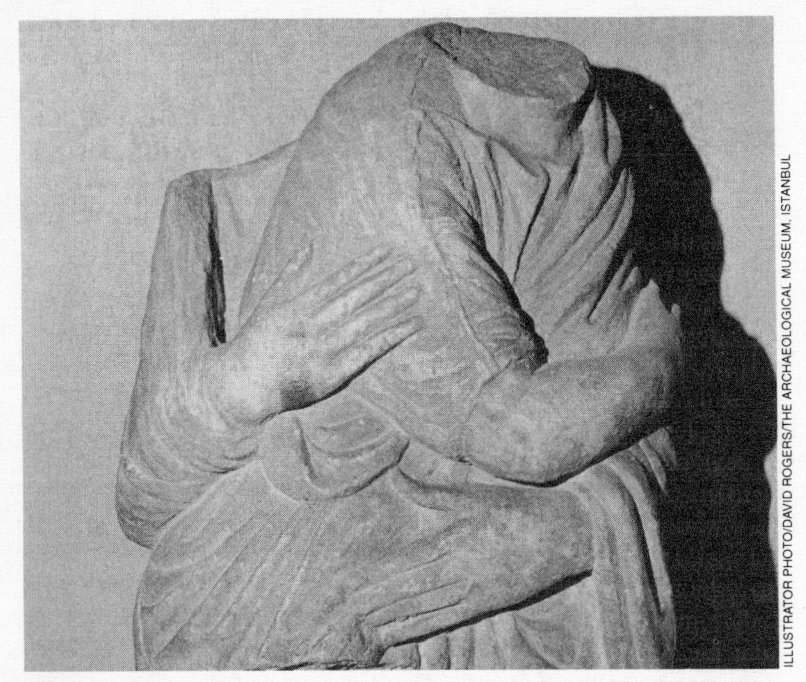
ILLUSTRATOR PHOTO/DAVID ROGERS/THE ARCHAEOLOGICAL MUSEUM, ISTANBUL

A torso statue of a man and woman embracing illustrates God's ideal of love between husband and wife. Hosea loved Gomer, forgiving her sins against him.

would "break the bow of Israel in the valley of Jezreel" (v. 5). The *bow of Israel* refers to the nation's military might. Reference probably is to the Assyrians destroying the army of Hoshea, the last king of Israel, in the valley of Jezreel before they besieged and destroyed the city of Samaria.

God told Hosea to name Gomer's second child *Lo-ruhamah*. Be careful not to misunderstand God's statement: "I will no longer have compassion" (v. 6). The point is: God's forgiveness when spurned has its limits (see Amos 2:6-16). For nearly two hundred years, God in His mercy withheld His judgment upon the wicked Northern Kingdom. It began with the reign of Jeroboam the son of Nebat around 931 B.C. and ended in sin in approximately 722 B.C., the ninth year of Hoshea's reign.

During these years, God reached out to the people of the

Northern Kingdom in love through the prophets, but they refused to hear. The cup of their iniquity and the resultant cup of God's wrath overflowed. God would now sweep them away as a nation (see 2 Kings 17:1-41).

Consequently, God commanded Hosea to call the second child—a girl—*Lo-ruhamah*, meaning "not pitied," to show that God would no longer extend "compassion" (mercy and grace) to the wicked people, but would utterly take them away.[1]

However, God continued to show mercy and grace to Judah, the Southern Kingdom, which had from time to time experienced revivals of true religion under the leadership of the prophets and godly kings (v. 7). God's salvation of Judah would not be "by bow . . . or horsemen," but "by the Lord." Reference is probably to God miraculously saving Judah and Jerusalem from the Assyrians in response to Hezekiah's turning to the Lord for help. (See 2 Kings 19:1-37, especially v. 35.)

God told Hosea to name the third child—another son—*Lo-ammi*, meaning "not my people." The name illustrated that, just as Hosea could no longer treat Gomer as his wife, God would no longer treat the Northern Kingdom as His people (vv. 8-9).

God's Word of Reassuring Hope (1:10—2:1)

God in His redeeming love would yet find a way to produce in Israel faithfulness to Himself. Then He would fulfill in and for them all of His covenant promises. In 1:10—2:1, God used strong, prophetic language to express His future blessing upon a united Israel. The expression "the sons of Israel" (vv. 10-11) refers to those of the ten tribes that God was about to destroy as a nation. The expression "the sons of Judah" refers to those who were loyal to the house of David.

"Yet" (v. 10) introduces the new day that God promised to bring to pass for Israel. First, God would raise up an unnumbered multitude who would be His true children (v. 10). God's scattering them in judgment would result in their being forcibly removed from the land God gave them for an eternal inheritance (see Gen. 12:7; 17:7-8; 2 Kings 17:6,23). God, in faithfulness to His promise, would bring them back into the land.

Second, God would unite them under "one leader" whom they would choose for themselves. That "one leader" is later identified as "David their king" (3:5; see also Jer. 30:9), whom we know to be the Second David, even the Lord Jesus Christ (Acts 2:22-36; 15:15-18). Thus, the ten tribes would be restored to the house of David. (See 1 Kings 11:39; 2 Kings 17:19-23).

Third, God would cause them to flourish in the land as His people. *Jezreel* (v. 11) would then take on a new meaning. It would no longer refer to God's scattering them in judgment (1:4-5) but to God's planting (sowing) them in mercy and grace. "And they will go up from the land" (v. 11) seems to point to their resultant prosperity in the land (14:5-8; Amos 9:13-15). However, some interpret "the land" (also "in the place," v. 10) to be the land into which God scattered them. "And they will go up from the land" then would mean their coming out of the place of scattering to flourish in the land of promise.

To affirm the reality of God's promises, Hosea pictured in his mind the redeemed nation and commanded them to speak to one another as brothers and sisters in the Lord (2:1). Their loving oneness with God under the rule of the Second David will bring loving reconciliation to divided and hostile Judah and Israel. They now would lovingly speak of each other as *Ammi* ("my people") and *Ruhamah* ("ones who have experienced together the mercy and grace of God").

As with all the Old Testament, the promises about Israel's future must be viewed in light of the New Testament. Christians agree that the promises are fulfilled in and through Jesus Christ. Most Christians also agree that Gentile believers are included among God's people. Not all Christians agree about whether the physical descendants of Israel have a special future in God's coming kingdom. Some Christians see the promises completely fulfilled in a spiritual Israel of Jewish and Gentile believers. Other Christians insist that some of the Old Testament promises must be fulfilled to physical Israel. The former group quotes passages like Romans 9:26 where Paul quoted Hosea 1:10 to show that the people of God include Gentile and Jewish believers. The latter group points to Romans 11:25-26 to show that God promises a future for physical Israel.

Lessons for Life from Hosea 1:1—2:1

When studying the Bible, we must interpret carefully its meaning and diligently apply its message to life today. Careful interpretation involves seeking to understand the meaning of the Bible text to the human author and first readers. Diligent application involves letting the eternal principles in the Bible text speak to our own lives.

The first objective in studying the Book of Hosea, therefore, is to understand the message God spoke to Israel through Hosea. Much of the content of this textbook is to help achieve this objective. The second objective in studying Hosea is to hear and respond to what God says to us through this portion of His Word. Applications or lessons for life are suggested as a part of each chapter of the textbook.

Here are some lessons for life from Hosea 1:1—2:1:

Sin is basically against God and His love.—Some people think of sin as if it were a brave rebellion against a heavenly tyrant. The false gods of pagan religion were portrayed as powerful but fickle deities; therefore, humans who defied these tyrants were often considered heroes. By contrast, God is love. Sin is rejection of love. Sin grieves God's heart just as Gomer's unfaithfulness grieved Hosea's heart.

Sin brings destruction.—Adultery destroys families today as Gomer's adultery destroyed her family. Sexual sins destroy nations today as the Israelites destroyed their nation by turning from God to live according to the licentious practices of the fertility gods.

God's Word brings life.—Tragedy can open hearts to God's Word as marital heartbreak opened Hosea's heart to the message of God's redeeming love. You can find in God's Word power to live again in the same way Hosea found power in God's Word to redeem his home.

Putting God first brings love and unity.—We become like the God or gods we worship. Israel became like the destroying fertility gods she worshiped. In contrast, Betty and I experienced love and oneness in our home by focusing on God with all of our hearts. In the same way, divided and hostile people will find in God unity and love for one another when they choose the Lord

Jesus Christ as their one and only leader.

---

1. For a detailed discussion of the fall of the Northern Kingdom, see John H. Traylor, Jr., *Layman's Bible Book Commentary*, vol 6, *1 and 2 Kings and 2 Chronicles* (Nashville: Broadman Press, 1980), 84-86.

Personal Learning Activities

1. List the two divisions of Hosea. ______________________
2. Hosea prophesied to the ______________________ Kingdom.
3. Hosea prophesied during the reigns of: __________, __________, __________, __________, __________.
4. Whose prophetic ministry paralleled that of Hosea? ______________________
5. God used Hosea's ______________ to communicate His word.
6. List two interpretations for "wife of harlotry." ______________________
7. Define: *Jezreel*, *Lo-ruhamah*, *Lo-ammi*. ______________________
8. How did God use the names of Hosea's children as vehicles of revelation? ______________________
9. What three things did God promise in Hosea 1:10—2:1? ______________________
10. List one lesson you learned from this chapter. ______________________

Answers: 1. Hosea's marriage (1—3) and message (4—14). 2. Northern. 3. Uzziah, Jotham, Ahaz, Hezekiah, Joash. 4. Isaiah. 5. marriage. 6. chaste at time of marriage but later turned to other gods; at time of marriage, she was a prostitute or young lady who sacrificed her virginity with Baal priests. 7. "the Lord sows or scatters"; "not pitied"; "not my people." 8. pointed to judgment on Israel for sin and to the redemption of God's love. 9. raise up a multitude to be His true children; unite them under one leader; let them flourish in the land. 10. personal answer.

2

GOD'S QUEST TO REDEEM ISRAEL

Hosea 2:2-23

John Green told about an almost unbelievable experience that illustrates the power of God's redeeming love. During the Korean war, an American soldier left behind his loving wife to go fight for his country. They daily wrote of their love for one another, but then his letters stopped. She continued to write in hopes that all was well. But one day the sad news came; her husband had found a Korean woman whom he loved, and he planned to stay with her in that country after the war. The brokenhearted wife remained faithful to her husband and sought to keep in contact with him as best she could.

Then news came from the Korean woman. She first told of the husband's illness. Her next communication told of his death and remarkable request. Would the American wife let the Korean woman and her two children (by the husband) live with her in America? The problem was their rejection in Korea because of the illegitimate nature of his relationship with the Korean woman. The husband wanted them to have a better life in America.

Could the American wife possibly take them to live with her? With a prayer in her heart, she sent the plane fare for the Korean woman and her husband's two sons. But how would it be when they met? The plane landed with the Korean woman and her two boys. The miracle of God's grace took place. Both women wept as they embraced. An outcast woman and her two small boys found a new home through the godlike forgiveness of an American woman.[1]

How would you react under the same circumstances? To what lengths will we go to redeem others? We thank God that

He does all that love in its fullness can do to redeem every person. His victorious quest to redeem unfaithful Israel illustrates the triumph we can experience through God's redeeming love. This is the theme of Hosea 2:2-23.

The great message of Hosea is God's persistent quest to redeem Israel from her sinful ways. God's persistent love for sinners is a theme that runs throughout the Scriptures. This good news is presented most clearly in the New Testament, which tells how God so loved the world that He gave His only Son (John 3:16), how Christ came to seek and save the lost (Luke 19:10), and how God revealed His love in Christ's death for us while we were yet sinners (Rom. 5:8). Nowhere in the Old Testament is God's love for sinners presented more clearly than in Hosea.

Summary of 2:2-23

Hosea 2:2-23 is what we call prophetic symbolism. Against the background of Gomer's unfaithfulness to Hosea, this passage tells the story of Israel's spiritual harlotry against the Lord God of Israel and the steps He would take to redeem them.

The prophecy pictures a husband, his wife, their children, and the wife's illicit lovers. The Lord God of Israel is the faithful husband. Israel is His unfaithful wife. Israel represents the people as a whole (corporate Israel) and at times the land. The children are the individual Israelites who are guilty of personal harlotry and thus are under God's judgment. The lovers represent the Baals.

Practical divorce between God and Israel occurred in the same way that Hosea put away his unfaithful wife. The names of Gomer's children told the story. Israel was no longer God's people ("Lo-Ammi," 1:9). God would no longer show them mercy and grace ("Lo-ruhamah," 1:6). Rather, He would now judge them for their sin ("Jezreel," 1:4-5).

God's judgment of Israel would be two-edged: punitive and redemptive. Through judging Israel for their sin, God would find those Israelites who would respond to Him in steadfast and righteous love. These He would redeem in complete fulfillment of all of His covenant promises to Israel.

God's quest to redeem harlot Israel would involve contending with her (vv. 2-5), chastising her (vv. 6-13), wooing her (vv. 14-15), remarrying her (vv. 16-20), and blessing her (vv. 21-23).

Contending with Unfaithful and Stubborn Israel (2:2-5)

How do you reach a mate who is stubbornly involved in adulterous relations? God's first step to redeem Israel was to plead with her to turn back to Him lest she reap the terrible consequences of her sin. But in her determination to pursue other lovers, Israel rejected God's plea and warning.

Pleading (v. 2)

This verse pictures a courtroom scene in which God is the Person who brings the suit, prosecutes the suit, and is judge and jury in deciding the suit's outcome. Israel's guilt was clearly established. God did not seek divorce from, but reconciliation with unfaithful Israel. However, reconciliation could not come until Israel put away her lovers (Baals) and embraced the Lord God in steadfast and righteous love.

God, under the figure of faithful Husband and Father, pleaded with the children to contend with their mother in order that she put away her harlotry and its external signs. The contending children are individual Israelites, most likely those like Hosea who had not worshiped Baal (1 Kings 19:18). These were faithful to worship God according to the law of Moses.

Contend is a strong word that pictures striving with words and even with blows to bring people to their senses. "Her harlotry from her face" and "her adultery from between her breasts" may be a graphic description of illicit sex. On the other hand, the reference may be to the jewelry worn in Baal worship. Or again, perhaps these were outward signs marking a woman as a harlot for hire.

Warning (vv. 3-4)

God instructed Israel with a sixfold warning of judgment. If Israel would not turn to God from her spiritual harlotry, God would: "strip her naked," "expose her as on the day when she was born," "make her like a wilderness," "make her like desert land," "slay her with thirst," and no longer have compassion upon individual Israelites who were guilty of harlotry.

The meaning of these judgments is that God would no longer show compassion on idolatrous Israelites but would put them to open shame. He would devastate their land and make them again as when He found them—a nomadic people, outcast in bondage and ready to die (Ezek.16:4-8). God's judgment would indeed be serious, but it would be merciful. He would not slay His adulterous wife as prescribed by the Law (Lev. 20:10; Deut. 22:22).

Rejecting God's Plea (v. 5)

The nation as a whole was fixed in Baal and calf worship. "I will go after my lovers" shows strong determination. They stubbornly rejected God's love because they were totally confused about the true source of life and blessings. They had accepted the lie that the Baals provided all the good things of life. Thus Israel had turned from the Lord to other lovers, whom she believed would provide food, clothing, and happiness.

People today do not worship the ancient Baals, but many are just as confused about the source of true life and blessings. Many non-Christians resist turning to Christ because they fear that the Lord will rob their lives of happiness. They believe that the world, not God, offers the good life.

Breaking the Heart of Unfaithful and Stubborn Israel (2:6-8)

"Therefore" introduces God's first action to make teachable the stubborn heart of unfaithful Israel. "Behold" points to the amazing nature of His action. He would fence them in with a thorn hedge. The thorn hedge reminds us of the shepherd's practice of using a thorn hedge to lead the sheep in the desired path.

Three good results would come from God's hedging the Israelites into a certain path. First, they would no longer be able to find "her paths," that is, the way to the Baal shrines. Second, the Israelites, in pursuing and seeking the Baals, would not be able to overtake or find them. The third is the best result: the Israelites would now understand that they had a better life when they looked to the Lord God of Israel to meet their needs. Thus, the people of Israel would determine to go back to the Lord, their "first husband" (v. 7).

After this first wave of judgment the Israelites would still be confused about the source of the good life. They would not yet know that all their blessings, attributed to Baal, came from God (v. 8). The people of Israel would not yet love the Lord with all their heart.

Teaching the Heart of Unfaithful and Ignorant Israel (2:9-13)

The often repeated story of the shepherd who broke the leg of the rebellious sheep to teach it love and obedience illustrates God's purpose and method in dealing with unfaithful Israel. The rebellious sheep not only went away from the shepherd but also led other sheep astray. When all other corrective methods failed, the shepherd broke and reset the sheep's leg.

After isolating the sheep for a while, the shepherd returned to feed it. The sheep refused the food and sought to bite the shepherd. After another period of isolating the sheep, the shepherd came once again to feed the sheep. This time the sheep not only ate the food, but licked the shepherd's hand. The shepherd explained the end result: "When finished, this sheep was the most obedient and loving of all my flock."

"Therefore I will take back," signals the second wave of God's judgment to redeem Israel. Israel's turning from God to Baal caused a blindness in her heart. The result was her thinking that her blessings had come from her following the Baal fertility rites.

God threatened to take five steps to enlighten Israel. First, God would take His blessings from Israel (v. 9). God used "My" to show that the grain, the new wine, the wool, and the flax belonged to Him. By withholding blessings, God would teach that He alone is the source of every good gift (Jas. 1:17).

Second, God would expose and punish the Israelites' lewdness before all the Baal lovers to display their inability to provide for the people's need (v. 10). What God did in the days of Elijah and Ahab illustrates what God could do. He dried up the land with a drought and called for a test between Baal and Himself to show Baal's inability to produce the rain. Elijah repaired the altar to symbolize a return to the true worship of God, that is, according to the law of Moses. Then God sent the drought-ending rain at Elijah's request to teach the Israelites that the Lord alone is God and that they were to worship Him according to the law of Moses. (See 1 Kings 17:1—18:46.)

Third, God would put an end to the festal assemblies, which they held in Baal's honor (v. 11). God had established special times for celebration, rest, and worship. The Israelites of Hosea's day prostituted these days in the worship of Baal (see Isa. 1:13; Amos 5:21). Accordingly, God called them "her [Israel's] festal assemblies" (v. 11) and promised to bring their corrupt celebrations to an end (see Amos 8:10).

Fourth, God would demolish Israel's grape vines and fig trees (v.12a). The spiritually-blind Israelites interpreted these to be their "wages" for Baal worship (v. 12b). *Wages* here refers to the pay given a harlot for services rendered.

Prophets often announced God's judgments on Israel's agriculture. "And I will destroy her vines." (2:12)

Fifth, God would punish the people of Israel for their Baal worship. *Baal* worshipers used the term to mean "the head of, master, lord." The term designated Baal in the mind of Baal worshipers to be the head of all of the gods. The plural *Baals* reminds us that each shrine had its own name for Baal, such as Baal of Peor (Num. 25:3) and Baal of Berith (Judg. 8:33). In following after their Baal lovers, the Israelites had forgotten the Lord their God (v. 13).

Winning and Remarrying Israel (2:14-20)

The judgments of verses 9-13 were designed to bring Israel back to God. Verses 14-20 picture the positive steps God took to win Israel back. Just as God's chastisement would be in stages and would produce the desired results, even so His redemptive action would be in three stages and would produce the desired results.

The first stage would involve three steps and would result in Israel becoming God's wife once again (vv. 14-17). God would first "bring her into the wilderness." "The wilderness" may refer to a secluded spot suitable for wooing and winning. However, "the wilderness" probably means the land from which God drove them which He made a wilderness (v. 3). God would now bring them back to their land, which still would be desolate at the time of their return. But more than *a desolate place* is meant by "the wilderness." The circumstances in the desolate land would be like those days in the wilderness when Israel loved God and depended solely upon Him (13:5).

God's second step would be to woo Israel. *And speak kindly to her* is literally "and I will speak to her heart."

God's third step would be to give to Israel "her vineyards" from the desolate land. "Her vineyards" are those that God gave to Israel as His wife but took away because of her going after Baal. *The valley of Achor* (v. 15a) means "the valley of trouble." It symbolized sin and wrath. It takes us back to the destruction of Achan and his possessions, including his family, for his taking what God had cursed (Josh. 7). When Israel embraced the Baals, she took what God had cursed just as Achan did in taking the spoils of Jericho. Their sin had brought terrible destruction upon them, their children, and their land. But now God would make "the valley of Achor" as "a door of hope." Its transformation would be a token of the eternal blessings they would enjoy from now on.

The Lord would now receive His desired response from Israel. The Israelites' answer to His proposal for remarriage would be a glad yes, as Israel of old responded when God brought them out of Egyptian bondage and made them His wife. But this time there would be a difference. The Israelites would no longer be confused about Who God is or their relationship to Him. The people of Israel would call Him *Ishi* (v. 16), that is, "My Husband." They would no longer call Him *Baali* (v. 16), that is, "My Master," so as to identify Him with unholy gods. Rather "in that day," that is, in the day of the Israelites' complete salvation, they would know Him as the Holy God to Whom they respond in holiness.

Ishi in contrast with *Baali* carries a deeper idea. *Baali* ("my master") implies a mistress relationship involving slavery. *Ishi* ("my Husband") implies a willing, loving, intimate, marital relationship in which Israel would be God's helpmate.

As the result of this new relationship, God would forever remove from Israel the influence and even the remembrance of Baal (v. 17). The expression "declares the LORD" (vv. 13,16,21) underscores the absolute certainty of Israel's redemption, remarriage, and blessing.

The second stage of God's redemptive action would involve His removing the causes that devastated the people and their land and His establishing for them an environment of peace (v. 18). God's covenant with "the beasts . . . the birds . . . and the creeping things" would put them in harmony with the Israelites and their land. This covenant would reverse the beasts' judgmental role (v. 12). God also would begin the process of removing war from the land. Just as God would break Israel through war (1:5), in reconciling with Israel He would break all the weapons of war. The result would be His causing the people of Israel to dwell securely in their land.

The third stage of God's redemptive action would result in Israel's forever being God's faithful wife (vv. 19-20).

God personally addressed Israel as His chosen wife and explained to her the betrothal. He first emphasized the eternal nature of His union with redeemed Israel. The betrothal would be "forever".

Next, God emphasized the reason the union would be eternal. He would give as His betrothal gift to Israel those qualities necessary for Israel to be forever His faithful wife. He would betroth Israel to Himself "in righteousness and in justice, in lovingkindness and in compassion."

God emphasized the resultant faithfulness of Israel. Betrothal "in faithfulness" denotes loyalty and steadfastness in the marital relationship. *Faithful* is what God had been and would always be to Israel. As a result of God's betrothing Israel to Himself forever in righteousness, justice, lovingkindness, and compassion, Israel would always be faithful to God.

"Then you will know the LORD" is the climax of the betrothal and marks God's dwelling with Israel forever. Knowing the Lord is the opposite of forgetting the Lord. It involves being in the closest relationship with the Lord.

Blessing Redeemed Israel (2:21-23)

God continued to describe what would take place in the day of Israel's complete salvation. Israel's faithful response to the Lord would enable Him to respond to them at even greater levels of blessing.

God's response would be to provide all of Israel's needs. *Jezreel* (v. 22) would still be a name for God's people. Previously, it stood for breaking and scattering His rebellious people (1:4-5). Now *Jezreel* would denote God's bountiful blessing upon His faithful people whom He would sow in the land that He had given for their eternal possession.

Israel's oneness with God would produce harmony between Israel and the universe. The result would be Israel's needs supplied. Jezreel's need would be signaled through the whole universe all the way up to God. God would then respond to the heavens, the heavens to the earth, the earth to crops, and the crops to Jezreel's intercession to God for her needs to be met.

God would also change the other names for Israel to symbolize His blessing them. *Lo-ruhamah* ("no compassion") would be changed to *Ruhamah,* for the Lord would "have compassion on her who had not obtained compassion" (v. 23b). *Lo-Ammi* ("not my people") would be changed to *Ammi* ("my people"), for redeemed Israel would be God's people (v. 23c). Their response—"Thou art my God"—would then be not in word only but in steadfast and righteous love.

With the expression "declares the LORD" (v. 21a), God underscored the certainty of this day of future blessing. In shedding His blood, the blood of the new testament (covenant), Jesus made possible this new relationship for everyone of Israel and indeed for everyone of all peoples who will believe in Him (Matt. 26:28).

Lessons for Life From Hosea 2:2-23

Hosea 2:2-23 is much more than a study of ancient history. The same God who persistently sought to redeem ancient Israel is the God who seeks sinners through Jesus Christ. Hosea is frequently quoted in the New Testament. For example, both Peter (1 Pet. 2:10) and Paul (Rom. 9:25) apply Hosea 2:23 to what God has done in offering saving mercy to all people through Jesus Christ. The lessons from Hosea 2:2-23, therefore, apply to God's quest for lost and straying sinners. The responses called for by ancient Israel are lessons for life for sinners in every generation.

Hear God's call to repentance.—God calls us through His Word to turn to Him from sin, just as God contended with unfaithful Israel to turn them back to Him. Refusal to turn to God from sin brings severe consequences today just as in the case of the unrepentant Israelites.

Respond in love and obedience to God's chastisement.—God chastens us to teach us to love and obey Him as He chastened the people Israel to keep them from their Baal gods and to make them teachable. I heard a mother pray that her children would respond to God's gentle admonition through His Word so that God would not have to speak to them through harsh judgment.

Ask God to give you the heart to serve Him.—God speaks to our hearts as He did to the Israelites. Let us yield our hearts to

God. Then He will be able to give us hearts of steadfast and righteous love to serve Him in faithfulness forever.

Blessings follow reconciliation with God.—Responding to God in steadfast and righteous love puts us in harmony with God and His universe. Then God's blessings will flow into our lives without hindrance as in the case of the redeemed Israelites.

---

1. John Green, "Illustrating the Book of Hosea," *The Theological Educator*, New Orleans Baptist Theological Seminary, Fall 1975, 91-92.

Personal Learning Activities

1. Hosea 2:2-23 is an example of: ________________ .
2. Who are the husband, wife, children, and lovers? ______ , __________ , __________ , __________ .
3. God's judgment was twofold: ________________ and ________________________ .
4. List the five phases of God's redemption of Israel. _______ , _______ , _______ , _______ , _______ .
5. Why did God no longer have compassion (v. 5)? ________ ________________________ .
6. From where did people think their blessings came? _____
7. Baal worship assumed what two forms in the North? ________________ and ________________
8. Before marriage, Israel called God __________ meaning __________ . After marriage, Israel would call Him __________ , meaning __________ .
9. List the four qualities God gave to Israel which were necessary for an eternal relationship with Him. ________ , ________ , ________ , ________
10. What were Israel's new names and their meanings? ________________________ ________________________

Answers: 1. prophetic symbolism. 2. God, Israel, individual Israelites, Baals. 3. punitive, redemptive. 4. contend, chastise, woo, remarry, bless. 5. people fixed in spiritual harlotry. 6. Baal. 7. Canaanite Baal worship, calf worship. 8. Baali, My Master, Ishi, My Husband. 9. righteousness, justice, lovingkindness, compassion. 10. Jezreel—blessing God would sow; Ruhamah—have compassion on her who had not had it; Ammi—my people.

3

LOVE AS GOD LOVES

Hosea 3:1-5

Perhaps you have heard of a sleepwalker who overruled his friends' warning not to accompany them on a safari. Friends feared that his sleepwalking habit would get him into trouble. They were right! The first night in the bush they finally found him roaming in the wild with two ravenous lions about to pounce upon him. They turned away in helplessness with the remark: "Since he got himself into the trouble, he will have to get himself out of trouble."

Unlike the sleepwalker's friends, God is both willing and able to help us. Gomer, Hosea's wife, brought tragedy upon herself and her family by her adulterous life-style. She shattered her family and stood hopelessly enslaved in her sin and its consequences.

Hosea in himself was helpless to redeem his wife. But Hosea found both the desire and the power to redeem his wife from her adulterous life and its consequences by obeying God's command to love Gomer as God loves Israel. Hosea also found power to bring his wife to have steadfast love for him and their family.

God's Word is like a coin with two sides. One side is the divine truth, and the other side is our response to the divine truth. Hosea's redemption of Gomer illustrates that we can find power to redeem others, even a wayward mate, in obeying God's command to love as God loves. That is the divine truth. Our response is to be: "Go again, love. . . " (v. 1).

Summary of 3:1-5

Hosea 3:1-5 continues the prophetic symbolism by which God revealed His redeeming love through Hosea's marriage. "Go again, love a woman who is loved by her husband, yet an adulteress" is God's third command to Hosea in relation to Hosea's family. In each case the prophetic symbolism involved God's command to Hosea, Hosea's execution of the prophetic act, and then the interpretation of the act for Israel.

God first commanded Hosea to take to himself a wife in the same way that God had chosen the Israelites to be His people (1:2). Hosea chose Gomer (1:3) who, like the people of Israel, committed "flagrant harlotry, forsaking the Lord" (1:2).

God next commanded Hosea to name the children of Gomer to picture the tragic consequences of Israel's sin (1:4-9). However, God also used the children's names in His prophetic word (1:10—2:23) to symbolize His future redemption of Israel. At that time Israel would once again be God's people to whom He would show compassion and upon whom He would bring bountiful blessing.

Hosea personally described God's third command to him (v. 1). In obedience to God's command, Hosea bought Gomer back for himself (v. 2) and placed her in the disciplined life-style necessary to turn her from harlotry and to win her to himself in faithful love (v. 3). The triumph of God's love in redeeming Israel "in the last days" (vv. 4-5) implies that Gomer did ultimately give herself willingly in steadfast love to Hosea and their family.

God's Command to Love as He Loves (3:1)

"Then the LORD said to me" indicates that the initiative to restore Gomer came to Hosea from God. Hosea's act of redeeming Gomer was rooted in and stemmed from God's redeeming love. "Then" ties God's command (for Hosea to love as God loves) to the redemptive actions of God toward Israel that were enumerated in 2:2-23. Thus, Hosea's actions toward Gomer would symbolize how God still loved the unfaithful Israelites and would take steps to redeem them completely unto Himself.

The word *again* is emphasized in the Hebrew text to denote God's call for persistence in Hosea's going and loving Gomer. "Go again" implies that Hosea had gone before—perhaps often—to Gomer in his attempt to redeem her. (See 2:2.) God through Hosea would now bring about a new day in the life of Gomer in the same way He would bring about a new day for unfaithful Israel. Perhaps the terrible consequences of Gomer's adulterous life had prepared her to respond in gratitude to Hosea's redemptive action. Certainly, God's chastisement of unfaithful Israel would prepare her to return to the Lord (2:7), to respond to the Lord (2:15), to acknowledge the Lord as her husband (2:16), and to confess the Lord as her God (2:23).

"To love" has many meanings. Modern people speak of "falling in love," "being in love," "making love," "showing love," and "feeling loved." The love God commanded Hosea to demonstrate toward Gomer was redeeming love. Hosea was to love Gomer as the Lord loved Israel. Such love is not expressed in feelings, words, or pious platitudes, but in redeeming actions (see Jas. 2:16; 1 John 3:18). The key idea in redeeming love is choosing to do good toward another even when the desired response is not forthcoming. Redeeming love expresses itself in establishing and maintaining loving relationships (11:1; 14:4). In verse 1 redeeming love would be Hosea's obedient action to win back his wife.

Who was the woman Hosea was to love? The same Hebrew word is translated "woman" here and "wife" in 1:2. However, the indefinite "a woman" plus the failure to name Gomer specifically have suggested to some interpreters that Hosea was to love a woman other than Gomer. But the use of "again" in the command "go again, love" clearly implies Gomer. Moreover, the analogy between Gomer/Israel and Hosea/God makes no sense unless Hosea went again in love to redeem Gomer just as God would go again in love to redeem Israel.

The Hebrew word translated "husband" is the general word for companion. Depending upon one's interpretation, the word could mean "friend" (KJV), "paramour" (RSV)[1], "another" (NIV)[2], or "husband" (NASB). Some interpreters assume that the companion of verse 1 was someone other than Hosea; however, the analogy between Gomer/Israel and Hosea/God suggests "husband" as the proper meaning. Hosea—Gomer's husband—continued to love unfaithful Gomer just as the Lord—Israel's husband—continued to love unfaithful Israel. The verbal form of "loved" denotes steadfast, unfailing love.

"Yet an adulteress" is what Gomer was in going from Hosea to give herself to other lovers. She was steeped in unfaithfulness to Hosea, but Hosea was steeped in love toward her. What an impasse! Could Hosea's love, fueled by God's love, transform her adulterous heart?

Israel did not deserve God's love any more than Gomer deserved Hosea's love. But God loved them and would redeem them in spite of their turning from Him to follow other gods. The expression "and love raisin cakes" describes the reason for their apostasy. "Loving raisin cakes" is equivalent to loving sexual sin. "Raisin cakes" were dried raisins pressed together for sweetmeat. Participants in the licentious Baal rites ate "raisin cakes." These delicacies symbolized to them the sweetness of their participation in the Baal fertility rites to satisfy their lusts and to increase productivity throughout the land in every area of life. Such sin may indeed be sweet for a season like "raisin cakes" in the mouth, but it turns within the stomach "to the venom of cobras" (Job 20:14).

Obeying God's Command To Love As He Loves (3:2-3)

"So" (v. 2) introduces Hosea's redemptive action to redeem Gomer in response to God's command. Conceivably, Hosea found Gomer for sale in the slave market. She had become the legal property of another man. Imagine the degraded state in which Hosea found her.

A further distinction needs to be made between feeling and choice in redemptive love. We have learned of Hosea's love for Gomer, but we need to ask about Hosea's feeling toward Gomer. She broke his heart and their family. She disgraced herself and him. She now was the degraded property of another man. How did Hosea feel toward Gomer?

Obviously, we do not know how Hosea felt. We, like Hosea, are to obey God's command to "go again, love," regardless of our feelings. A young lady, called of God to go to China as a missionary, shared with Dr. C. I. Scofield how obedience to God's command led her to love the Chinese. When she came to tell him good-bye, Dr. Scofield said to her: "I am so glad you love the Chinese well enough to give your life to them." But she said: "Oh, Dr. Scofield, don't you make any mistake. I don't love the Chinese. . . . I rather dislike them." "Why then are you going?" asked Dr. Scofield. She responded: "Because I love my Lord, and He has told me to go."

Where do the loving feelings enter? The young missionary returned seven years later on her first furlough to say to Dr. Scofield that she now loved the Chinese people and did not want to return home on furlough.[3]

Hosea acted in love toward Gomer in obedience to God's command. He bought her back and put her in a disciplined life to await love's response. By and by the feelings of steadfast love came—in Hosea's heart for Gomer and in Gomer's heart for Hosea.

Buying Gomer Back (v. 2)

Obeying God's command cost Hosea. However, not everyone interprets Hosea here as buying Gomer back. Some take verses 1-3 to be Hosea's personal description of how he carried out God's command in 1:2 to take for himself "a wife of harlotry." Such an interpretation makes Gomer a harlot when Hosea married her and the shekels and barley the price he paid to make her his wife. In other words, this view sees Hosea 1:2 and 3:1-3 as referring to Hosea's original marriage to Gomer, who—according to this view—was already a harlot. The main argument against this view is that Gomer did not again stray from Hosea after he redeemed her for himself. Also the word *again* in 3:1 implies something other than the original marriage.

The price Hosea paid to redeem Gomer for himself was "fifteen shekels of silver and a homer and a half of barley." The combined price is thought to equal 30 shekels, the price of a slave (Ex. 21:32). Most likely 30 shekels of silver was a large amount for Hosea to pay. The yearly wage paid to Micah's priest was 10 shekels plus his keep (see Judg. 17:10). Hosea's paying half the price in shekels and half in barley suggests that he scraped the bottom of his financial barrel to raise the redemption price.

Why was it necessary for Hosea to buy back Gomer? Interpreters suggest several possibilities. Some suggest that Hosea paid the money to Gomer's paramour to avoid an argument with him. Others say that Hosea provided the silver and barley for Gomer's upkeep until he would reinstate her as his wife. Yet others suggest that Gomer was a temple prostitute by vow, and that Hosea paid the 30 pieces of silver to release Gomer from her vow (see Lev. 27:4). The common view is that Gomer had become a slave-concubine and that Hosea paid the price of a slave to buy her back.

Hosea's payment of the redemptive price of a slave for Gomer reminds us of God's payment to redeem us. Our redemption cost a great deal more than 30 shekels. Our redemption came not by corruptible things such as silver and gold, but "with the precious blood of Christ, as of a lamb without blemish and without spot" (1 Pet. 1:19, KJV). Our redemption cost God His only begotten Son, the Lord Jesus Christ (see John 3:16). It cost the Lord Jesus His life (see 1 Pet. 2:24). Jesus' blood is the basis and the guarantee of the new covenant by which God put His law in the heart of believing Israelites and indeed in the heart of all believers of all time.

Winning Gomer Back (v. 3)

Hosea had bought Gomer back, but he had not yet won her back. Hosea accordingly placed Gomer in a disciplined setting in which she would have time to understand, to appreciate, and to respond in kind to his redeeming love. His actions symbolize the disciplined requirements of God's steadfast and righteous love toward Israel (v. 4) and indeed toward all humankind.

Hosea demonstrated the strength of redeeming love by the requirements that he placed on Gomer and on himself. With the statement, "You shall stay with me for many days," Hosea described the general conditions in which Gomer would live. *Stay* implies that Gomer should abide at home, devoted to household duties and shut off from would-be-lovers. "With me," literally "for me" (KJV), means that Gomer would live with Hosea in their home and be solely for him. "For many days" is emphatic in the Hebrew. It points to an indefinite and relatively long period of time. However, "for many days" is not forever. It points to a time when the purpose of the disciplinary period would be accomplished. There would be an "afterward" (v. 5) for Gomer as well as for Israel. Then Gomer would be ready, willing, and able to assume her position as Hosea's wife.

Hosea described three disciplines under which he and Gomer would live for a period of time. First, she would "not play the harlot," that is, Gomer would not go from Hosea after other lovers. Second, she would not "have a man." "Having a man" probably refers to sexual relations with any man. However, "a man" may refer to "a husband." Hosea had not redeemed Gomer for her to marry another. She would be for him alone. However, he would not have marital relations with her during this period. She would be without even her marital rights. Third, Hosea would have no connection with any other woman, but would keep himself exclusively for Gomer. Hosea would continue to keep himself pure and await the day when she in faithful love would come to him.

Victory in Loving as God Loves (3:4-5)

The text does not describe how Gomer responded to Hosea's actions. But the ultimate victory of God's love for Israel in verses 4-5 clearly implies Hosea's personal victory in his redemptive actions toward Gomer. After the discipline of the "many days," Gomer would return in her heart and seek Hosea in love as the Israelites would "return and seek the LORD their God and David their king." She would tremble in amazement at the power and goodness of God's love experienced in Hosea in the same way that Israel would "come trembling to the LORD and to His goodness in the last days." In this full union their home would become a beautiful illustration of God's redeeming love.

Love's Discipline for Israel (v. 4)

Hosea placed Gomer in the disciplined life-style described in verse 3 for two reasons. The first was to provide the circumstances most helpful to Gomer's responding in faithful love to his redemptive actions. The second reason ("for," v. 4) was to convey through prophetic symbolism the deprivation into which God would bring Israel. As in Gomer's case, these circumstances would lead the unfaithful Israelites to respond in faithful love to God's redemptive actions.

"The sons of Israel," here as in 3:1, most likely refers to the people of the Northern Kingdom. The cause of their losses would be the terrible desolation that God would bring upon them for their sin. The desolation would result in their remaining "without king or prince, without sacrifice or sacred pillar, and without ephod or household idols."

"Without king or prince" means that the Northern Kingdom would lose their entire royal institution. Israel's kings and princes symbolized the nation's rebellion against the Lord. God created His people to be a theocracy, that is, a nation over whom God Himself would rule. The appointment of a king came as the result of the people's sinful desire to be like other nations (1 Sam. 8:5-9). But God raised up David to be king. David was a man through whom God could and would accomplish His will (1 Sam. 13:14). Thus, God promised to establish forever the throne of David over His people (2 Sam. 7:12-16). God Himself would reign over His people in the Person of the Son of David (Luke 1:32-33; Rev. 22:3).

As the result of Solomon's sin (1 Kings 11:9-13), the ten northern tribes revolted from the house of David and established their own nation (1 Kings 12:16-20). The separation was not to be forever, but to chasten the house of David (1 Kings 11:39). Jeroboam the son of Nebat rejected God's offer to establish his house over the Northern Kingdom for the duration of the chastisement (1 Kings 11:26-38). Rather than give to God the required obedience, Jeroboam chose to establish the golden calf worship as the state religion of the Northern Kingdom (1 Kings 12:25-33). Each king followed the sinful practice of Jeroboam the son of Nebat. They heaped sin upon sin until God decided to destroy their kingdom. The destruction would result in their being without kingly leadership until they would "return and seek the LORD their God and David their king" (v. 5).

"Without sacrifice or sacred pillar" means that God would destroy their corrupt worship practices and leave them without true worship practices. The sacrificial system was sacred. Israel had corrupted the system by joining it with the practices of Baal worship.

"Ephod and teraphim" (v. 4, KJV) were means of discerning

God's will. The *ephod* was part of the priestly garment in which the lots were kept (see Ex. 28:6-35). *Ephod* at times refers to an image of wood covered with gold (see Judg. 8:27). "Household gods" (*teraphim*) were small sculptured figures falsely used as a means of seeking God's will (see Gen. 31:19,34). God would remove from them the false and deprive them of the true means of knowing His will.

How long would the deprivation last? As in the case of Gomer, we have the indefinite but relatively long period denoted by "many days." Some interpreters see "many days" as including the Assyrian Captivity, the Babylonian Captivity, and also the age-long desolation to which Jesus pointed (see Luke 21:24). The main point is that the period of deprivation would be as long as would be necessary to prepare "the sons of Israel" to return to God. The glorious fact is that the "many days" will come to an end and have an "afterward" when Israel will "return and seek the LORD their God and David their king" (v. 5).

Love's "Afterward" for Israel (v. 5)

God in His redeeming love will ultimately bring Israel back to Him and fulfill all of His redemptive purposes toward them. Each of the first three chapters of the Book of Hosea concludes with a prophetic description of Israel's full and final return to God (see 1:10—2:1; 2:14-23; and 3:5).

Afterwards focuses on the glorious salvation that God will bring to Israel after their "many days" of disciplined existence.

"Return . . . seek . . . come trembling" describe the spiritual renewal that God would ultimately bring to Israel. *Return* involves turning toward God that would result in their turning from other gods to give themselves totally to Him. The intensive nature of the verb *seek* shows the zeal and sincerity with which Israel will turn from disobedience to do the will of God. *Come trembling* is difficult to interpret. The idea seems to be that the Israelites' terrible judgment would cause them to fear God and to stand amazed at His goodness toward them. Part of their trembling would probably be fear lest they again attribute the goodness of God to some other god.

What or whom did Hosea mean by "David their king"? He probably did not mean David himself. Some think Hosea meant a Davidic king like Zerubbabel under whom all the tribes of Israel would unite. Other interpreters take Hosea to mean the Messiah, called the Second David, through whom God would fulfill His promise that the seed of David will reign forever on the throne of David. Certainly, the final fulfillment of Hosea's prophecy is in the Lord Jesus Christ (see Luke 1:32-33).

This prophecy will come to pass "in the last days." This expression is literally "the end of days." Some think Hosea meant only a period future to him. I agree with those interpreters who see the expression "the end of days" as beginning with the coming of Messiah and culminating with His Coming again. According to this interpretation, the people of Israel are seen during this period to be in rebellion against the Lord, to suffer greatly for their rebellion, and to return to the Lord from their rebellion. God's people will then be as one flock with God and the Davidic Messiah reigning over them.

Lessons For Life From Hosea 3:1-5

The key words in Hosea 3:1-5 are "love . . . as the Lord loves" (v. 1). This foreshadows the New Testament challenge for Christians to love others with the same kind of love in Christ that God has shown us. For example, Jesus told His disciples: "Love one another, even as I have loved you" (John 13:34). John emphasized that "we love, because He first loved us" (1 John 4:19). Concerning practical expressions of Christian love, Paul wrote: "Be kind to one another, tender-hearted, forgiving each other just as God in Christ also has forgiven you" (Eph. 4:32). Thus just as God's love for unfaithful Israel challenged Hosea to love unfaithful Gomer, so our own experiences with the God of love challenge us to love as God loves. What specific lessons about this kind of love are in Hosea 3:1-5?

Love is doing as God commands.—Christian love is primarily something we do, not something we feel. God commands us to do good toward brothers and sisters in Christ (John 13:34-35), all people ("neighbors," Luke 10:25-37), and even enemies (Matt. 5:43-47).

Love perseveres to redeem.—God's love does everything possible to seek to redeem sinners. Jesus, for example, told of a shepherd who seeks his lost sheep "until he finds it" (Luke 15:4). God's love seeks sinners all the way to the cross. When we love others with this kind of love, we must persevere in efforts to help. Where forgiveness is involved, we must not set limits on forgiving others (Matt. 18:21-35).

Love finds opportunity in tragedy.—People are open to being helped only when they are aware of needs they are unable to meet or problems they cannot solve. Therefore, when people hit bottom, they are often open to loving efforts to help them. The prodigal son, for example, did not begin to face reality until he found himself starving to death (Luke 15:17).

Love will win.—In his great chapter on love, Paul described Christian love and declared that "love never fails" (1 Cor. 13:8). Love is part of the eternal order of the God of love. When all the earthly ways of expressing loving service have come to an end, love itself will continue (1 Cor. 13:8-13). The triumph of love does not guarantee that every person will respond positively to God's love, but it does ensure that many will respond to God's love and that His loving purpose will triumph.

A positive response to love opens one's life to the blessings of loving and being loved.—Those who close their hearts to love condemn themselves to be unloved and loveless. Strictly speaking, they are not "unloved." God and others have offered them love, but they chose to be unloved by rejecting love. For love to work, it calls for a positive response. Those who receive and give love—whether to God or others—open their lives to the joys of being loved and loving.

---

1. Scripture quotations marked (RSV) are from the *Revised Standard Version of the Bible*, copyright 1946, 1952, © 1971, 1973.
2. Scripture quotations marked (NIV) are from the Holy Bible, *New International Version*, copyright © 1973, 1978, 1984 by International Bible Society.
3. G. Campbell Morgan, *Hosea: The Heart and Holiness of God* (New York: Fleming H. Revell, 1934), 26.

Personal Learning Activities

1. Gomer's redemption was rooted in: ________________
2. God's chastisement of the Israelites would prepare them to: __________, __________, __________, __________.

3. Write a brief description of *redeeming love.*

____

____

4. Explain Hosea 3:3b. ______________________________

____

5. Hosea paid ________ and ________ to redeem Gomer.
6. Why did Hosea discipline Gomer? _________________

____

7. Of what would Israel be deprived when disciplined? ____

____

8. After being disciplined, the Israelites would: ________, ________________, ________________.
9. Each of the first three chapters closes with: ________

____.

10. Identify one person to whom you need to express redeeming love and map out a step-by-step plan. __________

____

Answers: 1. God's redeeming love. 2. return, respond, acknowledge, confess. 3. a love that chooses to do good toward another even when the desired response is not forthcoming. 4. expresses apostasy and the reason for it. 5. fifteen shekels of silver, one and a half homers of barley. 6. to help her respond to his redeeming love and to convey symbolically what God would do unto Israel. 7. king or prince, sacrifice or sacred pillar, ephod or household idols. 8. return, seek, come trembling. 9. a prophetic description of Israel's return to God. 10. personal answer.

4

GOD'S CONTROVERSY WITH ISRAEL

Hosea 4:1-19

A minister friend saw in a dream the solution to the problems that are destroying our land, our homes, our churches, and our loved ones. In the dream Earl was meeting with a group of men. They entered the elevator and pushed the up button. To their surprise the elevator cleared the building and stopped only when it entered heaven. Earl explained that they did not see God. But they did see many heavenly beings talking together in groups. The heavenly beings sadly observed the affairs of people on earth. Each group had the same question: why don't you simply love and pray for one another? Earl woke up from the dream in a cold sweat. He has since seized every opportunity to convey the message of the dream. That message is: we can solve many of our problems by loving and praying for one another.

Why don't we love and pray for one another? The timeless message of Hosea tells us. Faithfulness and love are lacking because there is no knowledge of God (v. 1). "Swearing, deception, murder, stealing, and adultery" (v. 2) fill our land and destroy our homes because people do not personally know the Lord. A church marquee proclaimed: "No Jesus, no love; know Jesus, know love."

Even in our churches we often lack faithfulness and love to one another. A director of missions reported that one-third of the churches in his area are in turmoil caused by God's people not acting in love. We as God's people need to apply to our hearts the message, "Know Jesus, know love."

Summary of Hosea 4:1-19

The Book of Hosea is in two main parts: revelation through Hosea's marriage (chaps. 1—3) and revelation through Hosea's messages (chaps. 4—14). Hosea's messages as recorded in chapters 4—14 are hard to outline. Certainly, they focus on the broad themes of God's indictment of the people of Israel for their sin (4:1—7:16), of God's judgment upon the people of Israel for their sin (8:1—10:15), and of God's ultimate redemption of the people of Israel from their sin (11:1—14:9).

Hosea 4:1-19 is part of God's indictment of the Israelites for their sin. Hosea likely spoke these words at the city gate where the people had gathered to conduct civic and religious affairs. Included in the audience were prophets and priests, rulers, and other men. Included also were some people from Judah, the Southern Kingdom.

In this legal setting Hosea announced God's controversy with Israel. He condemned the people as a whole for polluting the land (vv. 1-3) and the priests and prophets for rejecting instead of teaching God's Word (vv. 4-6). Hosea further condemned the priests, the prophets, and the people for leaving God to follow the spirit of harlotry (vv. 7-10). He warned of the twin dangers of alcohol and sexual immorality (vv. 11-12), and he singled out the men for corrupting their wives and daughters (vv. 13-14). Hosea called upon Judah to learn from God's condemnation of Israel not to forsake the Lord to follow after other gods (vv. 15-19).

Condemnation for Polluting the Land (4:1-3)

Hosea contended with the people of Israel for their sin against the Lord as he encouraged his children to contend with his wife and their mother Gomer for her sin against him (see 2:2). *Case*, with its basic idea of striving or contending, is used here to refer to a legal suit. Hosea announced to the Israelites the findings of the heavenly court against them. God, the offended party, also served as Prosecutor and Judge.

The people of the Northern Kingdom possessed the land as a covenant gift from the Lord their God. But they had not given to Him faithfulness and love. Indeed, their actions toward Him could best be likened to Gomer's forsaking her husband, Hosea, to go after other lovers. In calling the people of Israel to "listen to the word of the Lord" (v. 1), Hosea encouraged them to turn to God for the adjustments in their life-style to correspond to His demands.

Israel's basic sin of forsaking God and following other gods had two tragic consequences. First, God could not find in the people the qualities of faithfulness, love, and knowledge of God that He required (v. 1b). Second, embracing other gods produced sins against God and their fellowman that resulted in much violence and bloodshed (v. 2). Their sin was so great that even nature was affected (v. 3).

What They Lacked (v. 1)

God's first charge against His people centered around the good qualities that He demanded but could not find. *Faithfulness* is the quality of being truthful, honest, loyal, and dependable in affections and actions. *Kindness* is the quality of being good and merciful in attitudes and actions. These qualities are necessary for a just society. Indeed, without these qualities society becomes fierce. *Faithfulness* and *kindness* describe how God relates to His covenant people and what He demands that they be to Him and to one another.

"Knowledge of God" is more than knowing facts about God. It is the intimate, personal experience with God that comes from obeying God's Word. Through knowing God, people come to be faithful and loving toward God and one another. The Israelites of Hosea's day were without *faithfulness* and *kindness* because they were without the knowledge of God.

Someone said of a famous politician of another generation: "He had all the qualities of a great statesman except two—ability and honesty." Presumably, the critic meant that the politician had charm and good looks but lacked the competence to do the job and the integrity to do it right. What a terrible indictment! He had everything except what he needed most.

Israel in Hosea's day had many outward marks of prosperity and success. Even their religious ceremonies were popular. But what they lacked were the essential qualities of being God's people: they didn't know God, and they lacked faithfulness and kindness in their dealings with one another.

All Kinds of Sins (v. 2)

God's second charge focused on the sinful actions by which the people polluted the land. Knowing God would have produced in the people *faithfulness* and *kindness*. Following "the spirit of harlotry" (4:12; 5:4) produced in them "swearing, deception, murder, stealing, and adultery" (v. 2).

Each of these sins violated the Ten Commandments, the fundamental principles God set forth through Moses to govern Israel's relationship to Him and others. Either in false *swearing* or cursing, the people took God's name in vain (Ex. 20:7). *Deception* violates the commandment not to "bear false witness against your neighbor" (Ex. 20:16). *Murder*, the unlawful and intentional taking of human life, breaks the commandment, "You shall not murder" (Ex. 20:13). *Stealing*, taking what belongs to another, violates the commandment, "You shall not steal" (Ex. 20:15). *Adultery* is the sexual relationship of a man with a woman who is not his wife, or vice versa. It breaks the commandment, "You shall not commit adultery" (Ex. 20:14).

"Swearing, deception, murder, stealing, and adultery" produced other sinful actions. Violence became a common practice among the people. The result was murder after murder until the blood of the victims ran together (v. 2b). The Israel of Hosea's day was indeed morally rotten and deserved God's judgment. The people had become like the Canaanites whose sin brought God's judgment and the loss of the land before the Israelites (see Lev. 18:24-25).

Environmental Crisis (v. 3)

Therefore (v. 3) points to the consequences of Israel's sin. The judgment perhaps took the form of terrible drought with attendant famine and pestilence (see Amos 7:6-13). The land had begun and would continue to wither until it would be incapable of supporting any form of life. Everything in the land would languish away. *Languishing* would continue until the animals, the birds, and even the fish of the sea were all gone.

Do not be surprised if Hosea 4:1-3 sounds like reading today's newspaper. Faithfulness and kindness are noticeably lacking. Deception, murder, stealing, adultery, and violence dominate the news. The environmental crisis has become so serious that it too makes the news.

The Bible says that all of these are evidences of an underlying problem: people do not know God. Many people turn up their noses at what appears to them to be a simplistic solution to a complex set of problems, but the prophets and preachers of God's Word have been much closer to the truth than the experts who analyze the human conditions without reference to the God who created us in His image. At the root of our moral, social, and environmental problems is the false and arrogant assumption that people today have outgrown any need for God.

We are like the spider in the old fable. He lowered himself by a single thread from the top of the barn and spun his web far below. There he lived and grew fat on the insects caught in the web. One day the spider noticed the single thread that extended up from the top of the web and disappeared into the darkness above. He wondered what good came from this old thread. So he cut it, and the spider and web collapsed in a heap on the barn floor.

Condemnation for Rejecting God's Word (4:4-6)

An unexpected visitor left a provocative question with the eight thousand preachers assembled in London, England, for their annual conference. The man drifted into the preachers' meeting to get out of the rain. He arrived during a question-and-answer period. When recognized by the chair for a question, he accused preachers with being like drones (bees who do no work but live off the labors of others). The visitor explained that he came from Sheffield where people were busy mining coal and making steel and had no time for religion. Then he asked the presiding preacher: "Are you productive?"

The implications of the question is that the ministry performed by preachers is of no practical benefit. You probably agree with Hosea and me that faithful preachers and teachers of God's Word are not only productive but indispensable to the well-being of humankind. Man does "not live on bread alone, but on every word that proceeds out of the mouth of God" (Matt. 4:4; see Deut. 8:3).

This does not mean that all who call themselves preachers are spiritually productive. Some are preachers of God's truth as Hosea was in his day. Others are like the many priests and prophets of Hosea's day who not only did not speak God's truth but actively rejected the truth.

God placed the blame for the Israelites' wickedness and impending national destruction squarely on the priests and the prophets. God concentrated in verses 4-6 on the priests because they were primarily responsible for teaching the law of God. But the priests had not taught God's law to the people as God established them to do.

Indeed, they were not true priests. Rather, they were the product of the calf worship Jeroboam the son of Nebat substituted for true Yahweh worship (see 1 Kings 12:25-33). They personally rejected God's word and ceased to share it with the people (v. 6b). As the result, God's people were being "destroyed for lack of knowledge" (v. 6a).

Verses 4-5 have been understood in more than one way. The main point seems to be the guilt of the religious leaders. The people themselves were guilty. They could not excuse their own sins by putting all the blame on the priests. However, the priests were especially guilty.

The priest, like the prophet, was supposed to represent God to the people and the people to God (see Ex. 7:1). The priest was God's spokesman. To reject the priest was to reject the Lord whose message the priest delivered. Those who rejected the priest were guilty of high-handed sin and were to be put to death (see Deut. 17:12). The priests, however, sinned at a higher level. They rejected the word that God gave to them and refused to carry that word to the people.

Hosea charged that the priests "rejected knowledge" (v. 6). This involves rejecting God's law by which the knowledge of God comes. The basic thought behind rejecting God's law is treating it lightly or even despising it. An example of rejecting knowledge was the way priests fulfilled their role. Their whole system was opposed to the Word of God which required: (1) God alone to be worshiped; (2) Only Levites to be priests; (3) Jerusalem as the only place where sacrifices could be brought; and (4) worship of God only according to the law of Moses and not according to the cult of the golden calves or of Baals. God's rejection of them as priests included His taking their life (v. 5; Deut. 17:12) and His cutting off their children from the priesthood (v. 6c). In declaring that He would destroy the priest's "mother" (v. 5), God probably meant His destruction of their whole ungodly religious system. The Assyrian captivity would be the means of this destruction.

Condemnation for Forsaking God (4:7-10)

When I preached on keeping the Ten Commandments, a young deacon said jokingly, "Well, at least I have not made any graven image." A person can commit idolatry without making a graven image. Idolatry is turning from God to embrace whatever we desire or honor more than obedience to God's Word (see John 5:44). Israel of Hosea's day committed idolatry by rejecting God and by embracing the licentious practices of calf and Baal worship.

Verses 7-10 continue to describe the priests' sins. However, God shifts from direct to indirect address. The background of the priests' increase in number and sin (v. 7a) was God's blessings upon Israel in answer to King Jehoahaz's prayer for mercy (2 Kings 13:3-7). God brought the desired deliverance from the Syrians through Jehoahaz's son, King Joash (2 Kings 13:22-25). Then God enlarged Israel's borders through Jehoahaz's grandson, Jeroboam, as Jonah prophesied (2 Kings 14:25-29). But the priests as well as the king and the people did not give glory to God for their deliverance and prosperity. Rather they credited their blessing to their worship of Baal. Therefore, God would turn the priests' "glory into shame" (v. 7b).

Verse 8 refers to a perversion of the requirement that priests eat the animal that was offered as a sin offering (Lev. 6:26). The implication is that the priests of Hosea's day were actually encouraging the people to increase their sins so that the priests would receive the greatest possible supply of sacrificial meat.

"Like people, like priest" (v. 9) means that the priests would not be spared in the coming judgment. Their greater responsibility would bring greater guilt. God's punishment for them would be proportionate to their wicked ways and deeds. Part of their punishment would be that their eating would produce hunger and their harlotry would produce barrenness (v. 10).

Condemnation for Following the Spirit of Harlotry (4:11-12)

In the statement of His controversy with the Northern Kingdom, God returned in verse 11 to direct address (see "My people," v. 12). God did not clear the people of guilt even though the priests were principally responsible for the land's wickedness. His condemnation focused on the people's licentious, superstitious, heathen practices. They turned from God and the truth of His Word and were borne away by "the spirit of harlotry" (v. 12b).

"Harlotry, wine, and new wine" are evils with a destructive nature (v. 11). These practices "take away the understanding," that is, the heart. The adage says, "First a man takes a drink, then the drink takes the man."[1] *Harlotry* refers to the overt act of fornication and prostitution. It also refers to Baal worship (1:2; 2:5,13), which promoted fornication and prostitution as a means of obtaining fertility. In the case of the Israelites, they believed that the fertility rites produced the great harvest of "new wine." Thus, in their longing for the largest possible harvest of "new wine," they turned more and more to the harlotry and wine of the fertility cults.

You can see why Baal worship was so attractive to ancient society. For one thing, it promised material success, which in those days was measured by a large family and a rich harvest. Second, the means of securing this success involved sex and alcohol.

These evils of sexual immorality and free use of alcohol fed on one another as they do today. Sexual lust can lead to the use of alcoholic beverage as a tool for conquest and debauchery. Alcohol attacks the higher functions of the brain. It removes godly inhibitions. As has been said, after the first drink a man struts like a peacock; the second makes him roar like a lion; after the third he behaves like a monkey; and the fourth causes him to wallow like a pig. Alcohol attacks the will and leads people to do and say things that otherwise would not be done or said.

Condemnation for Corrupting Others (4:13-14)

God condemned the husbands and fathers for corrupting their wives and daughters. "Therefore" (v. 13) points to the consequences of the men following the licentious practices of Baal worship. "Your daughters play the harlot" refers to the Baal bridal rites where a virgin would submit herself to the male temple prostitutes or to strangers to assure her fertility. "And your brides commit adultery" refers to their wives' participation in the fertility rites with and as temple prostitutes.

God would not have to visit special judgment upon the daughters and wives of the men (v. 14). Rather, their promiscuous activities themselves brought destruction. The daughters and the wives joined their fathers and husbands in going aside with harlots and participating in the fertility rites. The result was a breakdown of their morals. Sexual immorality spread from their Baal shrines to their towns and to their homes. Drunken debauchery became their way of life. It took away their hearts and destroyed them as a people.

In recent decades a sexual revolution has taken place in our land. Sexual standards have radically changed. Sexual immorality, of course, is nothing new; but behavior that was once considered immoral is now condoned. The situation today is similar to the sexual wilderness of Hosea's day. Women as well as men are swept along by our culture's powerful promotion of promiscuous sex as the key to the good life.

Sex was part of God's good creation. God's purpose in sex is not only for the propagation of the race but also for the stability of the home as the foundation of society. Sex is the ultimate means of bonding together a man and a woman. Through the sexual union of a husband and a wife, each makes a total commitment to the other in responsible love. They totally trust each other and assume full responsibility for their relationship.

Whatever perverts this good purpose is sinful and immoral. It is a sin against God, against ourselves, and against one another. Societies that become riddled with sexual immorality relegate themselves to the garbage heap of history.

Counsel Not to Be Like Condemned Israel (4:15-19)

In 4:15-19, God addressed both Israel and Judah. His main

ILLUSTRATOR PHOTO/DAVID ROGERS/THE NEGEU MUSEUM BEERSHEBA

The worship of Baal and other foreign gods by means of incense was often condemned by Old Testament prophets. "They offer sacrifices on tops of the mountains and burn incense on the hills." (4:13)

emphasis was to warn Judah not to be like wicked, condemned Israel. Against the background of Israel's sin and imminent destruction, God gave a threefold admonition to Judah. God first charged Judah not to be like Israel in her worship (v. 15); second, not to be like them in stubborn rebellion against God (v. 16); and third, not to associate with them lest they contaminate and destroy themselves (vv. 17-19). In verse 17 " Let him alone " carries the idea of abandoning Israel to her sin and judgment.

Hosea warned against going to Gilgal or Bethaven (v.15). Gilgal and Bethel were two centers of calf and Baal worship. Bethel was most prominent, being "a sanctuary of the king and a royal residence" (Amos 7:13). The Israelites had made Bethel ("the house of God") into Beth-aven ("the house of deception"). God had sought, as it were, to yoke the Israelites in the easy service of treading out the corn. There they could have eaten freely without a muzzle as they walked around the threshing floor. But Israel, kicking and backsliding like a stubborn heifer (see Deut. 32:15; Hos. 4:16, KJV), refused God's gentle yoke. Their nature could only be changed by harsh chastisement (see Jer. 31:18). Accordingly, God would put them in the hands of a foreign master who would force them to do heavy field work. The heavy yoke would gall and produce deep wounds. In the end Ephraim would be "a trained heifer that loves to thresh" (10:11).

"Ephraim is joined to idols" refers to Israel's stubborn attachment to idolatry. *Ephraim*, the dominant tribe of the Northern Kingdom, stands for Israel. Although married to God, Israel had forsaken God to live with other gods (see 1:2). "Let him alone" (v. 17) means to leave Israel to God's judgment.

God's warning to Judah assumed that Judah could learn from the destruction that came on Israel. Sadly, Judah failed to learn the clear lesson and followed Israel's road to destruction.

Those who refuse to learn the lessons of history are doomed to repeat them. History is littered with the wreckage of nations which have forsaken God and chosen the excesses of sin.

Lessons For Life From Hosea 4:1-19

A police officer reported on the ravages of crime in our city to a civic committee on which I serve. A leading banker sitting at my side said in joking seriousness: "If preachers were doing their job, we would not have so much crime." I said: "You are right. We have more crime, because we have less knowledge of God." He then said in good humor: "Let's move on before we get a sermon."

Real faith in God involves personal knowledge of God.—Many people claim to believe in God but have no personal relationship with God. They may know certain facts about God, but this cannot substitute for knowing God personally. Personal knowledge expresses itself in worship, prayer, trust, and obedience.

The basic sin of not knowing God results in the many sins that destroy individuals and society.—Western civilization has been compared to flowers that have been cut and placed in water. We have cut ourselves off from our moral and spiritual roots. For a while such a civilization can be sustained by the momentum of past spiritual vitality, but eventually it withers and dies—like the flowers cut off from their roots. The evidences of this deadly process are as apparent today as they were in ancient Israel: crime, violence, breakdown of the family, addiction, debauchery, pollution of nature and lives. At the root of these problems are people who have no personal knowledge of God.

Hearing and responding to God's Word is a crying need.—Those of us who believe God's Word must not only proclaim it to others but also obey it in our own lives. Christians live in a non-Christian society that needs the Word of life. If we expect the world to pay attention to the Word we teach and proclaim, we must conform our own lives to the Word.

People who indulge themselves in drunkenness and sexual immorality sin against God, others, and themselves.—Such people often try to rationalize their behavior by saying, "If what I'm doing is wrong, I'm hurting nobody but myself." Such people are only partly right. They are hurting themselves, but their actions also hurt many others.

We must reflect God's love in our families.—The breakdown of society begins with the family, and the foundation of the home is the marriage relation. In our day of unfaithfulness in marriage, people need to build their lives and families on faith and faithfulness. Basic to this is faithfulness and love in marriage.

1. John Bartlett, *Familiar Quotations by John Bartlett*, 15th ed., ed. Emily Morrison Beck (Boston: Little, Brown and Company, 1980), 646.

Personal Learning Activities

1. What is the site where the message in 4:1-19 was presented and who is addressed? ________; ________ ________
2. Who are: offended party, prosecutor, judge, defendant? ________, ________, ________, ________
3. What were the two consequences of Israel's sin of forsaking God and following other gods? ________ ________; ________
4. Define "knowledge of God" (Hos. 4:1). ________
5. Describe the judgment which God rendered in Hosea 4:3. ________
6. Who did God blame for Israel's sin and why? ________, ________; ________
7. The priests neglected knowledge, so they would be ________ ________ by God.
8. Define *idolatry*. ________
9. Harlotry refers to: fornication, prostitution, ________.
10. What were the 3 admonitions God issued to Judah? ________ ________, ________, ________.

Answers: 1. city gate; prophets, priests, rulers, other men, Judah. 2. God, God, God, Israel. 3. people lacked faithfulness, love, knowledge of God; violence, bloodshed. 4. intimate experience with God. 5. drought, famine, pestilence, infertility, bereavement, miscarriage. 6. priests, prophets; hadn't taught God's Word. 7. rejected. 8. turning from God to whatever is desired more than obedience to God. 9. Baal worship for fertility. 10. don't be rebellious, worship like Israel, associate with Israel.

5

ISRAEL'S REBELLION AND FALSE REPENTANCE

Hosea 5:1—6:11

Genuine Christian conversion results in living for Jesus. Whether the circumstances of conversion are dramatic or inconspicuous, the newly born child of God will ask, "What shall I do, Lord?" (see Acts 22:10). One lady said that her exciting and deeply moving conversion to Christ made her feel as if she had jumped six feet in the air. Her discerning friend, with a less dramatic but equally genuine experience, said: "It is not how high we jump, but how straight we walk once we hit the ground."

My conversion experience was not dramatic but was effective in turning me from my sin to serve Jesus with all my heart. The night I was baptized I felt uncertain and insecure. Had Jesus really saved me as He promised in His Word? Was I truly a Christian? Would I be able to hold out? Was I a hypocrite in claiming to be God's child? Would I go back to my sin as a hog returns to its wallow (see 2 Pet. 2:22)?

The day after I was baptized I talked as usual with the fellows in the engineering building at Louisiana Tech. Just as before, I cursed, but there was a difference. Deep in my heart I said: "Cursing is wrong, and God being my helper I will never curse again." God did help me through His Spirit and His Word. As a newborn Christian I laid aside the old life of sin in its many forms and began shaping my life to conform to God's Word. Today the insatiable desire of my heart is to be like Jesus and to share Him with others.

Summary of 5:1—6:11

5:1—6:11 is part of a larger section, 4:1—7:16, that focuses on God's indictment of the Israelites for their sin. Interspersed throughout are descriptions of Israel's guilt, punishment, and redemption. The main focus of 5:1—6:11 is upon the devastating judgment shortly to come upon Israel by which God would ultimately redeem the people from their sin. The guilt, judgment, and redemption included Judah as well as Israel (see 5:10,12-14; 6:4,11).

Repentance was still open to Israel (see 5:1), but Israel would not seize the opportunity to turn to God from sin. Israel's corrupt leaders had ensnared and exploited the people (5:1-2). The spirit of harlotry and pride possessed Israel and prevented the people from turning to God from their sin (see 5:3-7). Desolating judgment from within and without would destroy the Northern Kingdom and the wicked life-style of the people (5:8-14; see 2 Kings 17:1-23). Some of the people would eventually heed the call to true repentance (6:1-3). But their present stubborn rebellion and false repentance left God no choice but to bring upon them the purifying fires of holy judgment (6:4-11).

Announcing Chastisement (5:1-2)

"Show Dr. Traylor how you prepare yourself to learn." As Mrs. Betty Trimble spoke these words to her first-grade class, the children came to attention with their faces toward their teacher. They were ready to obey whatever command she spoke. One of Mrs. Trimble's teaching secrets was leading her students to prepare themselves to learn. I brought this experience back to my congregation. As I asked them to open with me God's Word, I shared my experience with Mrs. Trimble's class and then said: "Show the indwelling Holy Spirit how you prepare yourself to learn."

Israel's trouble was their unwillingness to learn. They would not even give God their attention. In verse 1 God used three different words ("hear," "give heed," "listen") in trying to get their attention. Hosea pointed once again to the leaders of the nation who were chiefly responsible for the sins of the people.

This time he cited the "house of Israel" and the "house of the king" along with the priests (v. 1). "House of Israel" probably means the common people and tribal leaders. "House of the king" included the king and his larger family. These leaders as God's representatives were responsible for life in the land. They could have saved the nation by repenting and leading the people back to God. Instead they used their position and the fertility cult to ensnare and exploit the people. These leaders would experience the worst judgment.

The wicked leaders had inspired *revolters* to go deeper in rebellion and bloodshed (v. 2). *Chastise* means "teach by judgment." God sought through chastisement to turn the revolters to Himself. He warned that He would take His chastisement to the deepest level.

Rebellion and Impenitence (5:3-7)

I probably would now be dead if I had not turned to God from my sin. I was involved in the same bad habits that took my father's life at the age of 48. As I pondered on my way, I knew that I needed to break from my sin. But I found myself helplessly enslaved. By God's grace I asked God to free me from my sin and enable me to trust Him. I prayed: "Please save me from myself that I may trust You." God heard my heart cry. In turning to God He freed me from my sin and enabled me to put my trust in Him.

Repentance is turning to God from our sin. Sin enslaves us, but God liberates us. In His liberating us, we find power to turn to Him with all our heart. But in their pride the Israelites were unwilling to turn to God for help (v. 5).

Israel did not know God but God knew Israel (v. 3). Beginning with "for" in verse 3, God cited five reasons why He would severely chastise Israel and ultimately Judah. These reasons may have been given to those in Hosea's audience who objected to the declaration that Israel deserved destruction.

The first reason was that Ephraim had played the harlot and Israel stood defiled. *Ephraim*, where the royal family and the most influential elders lived, was the name of the most influential tribe of the Northern Kingdom. Indeed, *Ephraim* stands at times for all the Northern Kingdom. In its moral corruption, Ephraim had defiled the whole nation. "To play the harlot" includes licentious acts but basically means to turn from God to follow after the golden calves and the Baals. Both of these cults involved defiling sexual acts in hope of producing fertility.

The second reason was that the Israelites' deeds would not allow them to return to the Lord their God (v. 4). The following factors were involved. In turning from God to follow after the fertility cults, the people of Israel had opened their hearts to the spirit of harlotry. In giving themselves to the fertility cults, the spirit of harlotry now possessed them. The spirit of harlotry now controlled their minds, their emotions, and their wills. Finally, the decisive factor was that they did not know the Lord. Therefore, they were left without God's help to heal the paralysis of their soul.

The third reason God would chastise Israel and Judah was their prideful rejection of God's appeal for them to turn to Him for help (v. 5). Some interpreters take "the pride of Israel" to refer to the Lord (7:10). The idea then is that God's judgment of Israel was His testimony against their sin. My own opinion is that "the pride of Israel" refers in this case to Israel's stubborn pride. The idea is that their pride testified against their turning to the Lord for help.

The fourth reason was that the Israelites turned to the fertility gods for help (vv. 5b-6). Israel and Judah had begun to unravel because of sin. The process of disintegration would continue until Israel was swept away. The people sought to heal their land by bringing flocks and herds to the fertility shrines. But they would not find God, for He had withdrawn Himself from them. The real tragedy is that their sin had so blinded them that they thought they were seeking God by the sacrifices and other rites at the fertility shrines.

God would ultimately withdraw Himself as well from Judah. Ezekiel prophesied that the Glory would depart from the mercy seat of the temple to its threshold and finally to the Mount of Olives where He would preside over Jerusalem's destruction (see Ezek. 8:4; 9:3; 10:18-19; 11:22-23). Ezekiel also saw the Glory present with His people in Babylon, reigning over the captivity to bring back a purified remnant (see Ezek. 1:4-28).

The fifth reason for the Israelites' coming destruction was their treachery against the Lord their God (v. 7). Israel as an unfaithful wife had betrayed God her faithful Husband by turning to the fertility gods. Children were born who continued and intensified Israel's sin. The result was the coming destruction and dispersion from the land.

Desolating Judgment From Within and Without (5:8-15)

In my backyard is the hollow stump of an oak tree. The tree died, and I cut it down. The stump shows that the heartwood was eaten out. What caused the tree to die? Two bad things happened. First, the high water table choked off the oxygen supply to the roots causing root rot. Second, my neglect of breaks in the joints enabled fungi to get inside. The result was slow death. If I had not cut down the tree, the wind could have blown it down on my house.

Israel was rotten at the heart. God's judgment would soon sweep the nation away. Blowing the horns and trumpets was to signal approaching invaders (v. 8). The background of the invasion may be the civil war that broke out about 735 B.C. between Israel and Judah. The judgment, however, seems to go beyond this civil war to the desolation of Ephraim that occurred with the Assyrians devouring the land (see vv. 7,9,11).

Gibeah, Ramah, and Beth-aven (a scornful name for Bethel) were all cities in the land allotted to the tribe of Benjamin. These cities were now part of Judah. "Behind you, Benjamin" probably means that the judgment would now break out to the rear of Benjamin. In the prophet's mind the Assyrians had already swept through Israel (Ephraim) southward to Judah. God's desolation would shock in its severity (v. 9). Ephraim would become a proverb of God's judgment upon sin in the lives of His people (see Deut. 28:37). *Rebuke* means "to prove and correct." Thus, the final outcome of God's chastisement would be salvation for all who open their hearts to Him.

God's message through Hosea was for all the tribes of Israel, not only for the ten tribes of the Northern Kingdom. The coming judgment was an established fact. God's chastisement

ILLUSTRATOR PHOTO/DAVID ROGERS/HAZOR MUSEUM

Israelites made trumpets from conch shells and blew them to sound an alarm. "Blow the horn in Gibeah, the trumpet in Ramah." (5:8)

would ultimately embrace all of His people. God also would punish the people of Judah (v. 10)—but not with destruction at that time. Their crime was utilizing Israel's downfall to extend their borders northward. Their sin of removing boundary marks brought them under the curse of God (see Deut. 27:17).

God viewed Israel's desolation as complete (v. 11). In verses 11-15, God underscored why and how He would crush Israel. Verse 11 stresses the Israelites' determination to follow the fertility cults. *Man's command* is a human statute in contrast with a divine statute. In spite of God's every attempt to turn Israel to true worship as prescribed by Moses, the people were determined to pursue the golden calves and Baals. Verse 12 shows that God's judgment was inherent in Israel's sin. Their forsaking Him to embrace the fertility cults ate out their hearts like devouring moths. God also saw "rottenness" consuming Judah. Verse 13 laments the people's unwillingness to turn to God for healing. In their desperate plight, the people turned to Assyria who was unable to heal them. The identity of "King Jareb" is not known. Some interpreters take *Jareb* to be a nickname for Tiglath-pileser whom God made to be His avenger against His people.

Verse 14 emphasizes that God Himself would punish Israel and Judah. God would use the claws and teeth of persecutors like the Assyrians to teach His people. But God Himself would destroy them as a wild animal tears a victim to pieces.

Verse 15 combines a message of judgment and hope. God would withdraw from Israel so that they eventually would earnestly see Him. Where is God's place to which He would go after removing Himself from His people and carrying them into captivity (v. 15)? Reference may be to His heavenly palace. The main point is that He would leave His people in the hands of their enemies to suffer the ravages of their sin without His help. God would return to them when they returned to Him in true submission. To earnestly seek God would bring about the dawn of a new day for the people.

Call to Repentance (6:1-3)

Serious Bible students are often puzzled by Hosea 6:1-3 in light of the verses that follow. Taken by themselves, verses 1-3 seem to express genuine repentance; but verses 4-11 reflect God's sharp condemnation of superficial repentance. This has led some interpreters to assume that although verses 1-3 were the right words to express repentance, the people who said the words really did not mean them. Another possibility is that the words of verses 1-3 represent the call to true repentance to which God's people eventually responded.

Personally I prefer the latter view. It takes into account the call to true repentance of verse 1-3 and the condemnation of shallow repentance in verses 4-11. Although the people of Hosea's day showed only shallow repentance, under the chastening hand of God His people would eventually hear and respond to the call to true repentance. The speaker in verses 1-3 may have been Hosea using these words to call the people to repentance. Or the speakers may have been the people themselves in the midst of God's desolating judgment coming to their senses and using these words to call one another back to God.

Whatever the case, one fact is clear: Israel and Judah of Hosea's day were far removed from the deep-seated repentance necessary for God to heal them. Their worst judgment was still ahead. However, God's chastisement would lead to true repentance and result in reunion and blessing.

The exhortation is in two parts: the call to return to the Lord (vv. 1-2) and the call to know the Lord (v. 3). *Let us return* is literally, "Let us turn around, be converted." The process of turning back involves changing the mind, producing changed attitudes and actions. These words present the people as determined to serve God with all of their hearts.

The word *return* or *turn* is the most common word for repentance in the Old Testament. It is the same word in passages like Ezekiel 33:11, in which God says: "I take no pleasure in the death of the wicked, but rather that the wicked turn from his way and live. Turn back, turn back from your evil ways! Why then will you die, O house of Israel?" To truly repent is to turn around—to turn to God from sin. Feeling sorry for one's sins is not enough by itself. Sorrow for sin must be the kind of convicting that results in a change of mind, heart, and life.

Verses 1-2 give assurance that God will receive truly repentant people. In accord with His purpose to heal, God had *wounded* His people. When they wanted to return, He would begin the process of comforting them in their distress.

The references to "two days" and "the third day" (v. 2) are figures for short periods of time. Once God began to comfort His people in their affliction, it would be a short time before they would begin to live again as God's people. By "the third day," God would have lifted them up from their fallen position and would have established them forever as His people. Then they would proceed to live out their loving and loyal devotion to Him as their God. This prophecy has its parallel in Ezekiel's vision of God raising up a mighty army from the valley of Israel's dry bones in order to serve His purposes (Ezek. 37:1-14).

The call to know the Lord involves determination, assurance, and blessing (v. 3). "Knowing the Lord" is the rich, personal fellowship with God that produces loyalty and love toward God and others. The determination "to know" and to "press on to know the Lord" arises out of the new life God gives to His people. The assurance of God's loving response to His people's desire to know Him is already established in nature. His going forth to meet His people in love is as certain as the coming of dawn after the night. His blessing them in that day is just as certain as the seasonal rains, especially the spring rain, which produces an abundant harvest.

Thus Hosea 6:1-3 sounds a call to true repentance, which includes the promise of divine forgiveness and new life. This is a familiar biblical theme. Hosea's contemporary, Isaiah, expressed a similar call: "Seek ye the Lord while he may be found, call ye upon him while he is near: Let the wicked forsake his way, and the unrighteous man his thoughts: and let him return unto the Lord, and he will have mercy upon him; and to our God, for he will abundantly pardon" (Isa. 55:6-7, KJV).

Judging to Produce Godly Knowledge and Loyalty (6:4-11)

An exasperated father said to his wayward son, "You would even wear God out!" God would one day receive from His people the glorious response described in 6:1-3. But what was He to do with Israel and Judah of Hosea's day?

You should read the two questions in verse 4 with a heavy heart in order to understand God's dilemma with the superficial dedication of His people to Him. Like an exasperated parent, He asked, "What shall I do with you?" In spite of God's every attempt to lead the people back to Himself, the people of both Ephraim and Judah remained superficial in their devotion to Him.

What apparently distressed God was the lack of permanence in the people's *loyalty* to Him and to one another. *Loyalty* is rooted in covenant love. It binds God to His people and His people to Him and to one another. This covenant love is rooted in and stems from God Himself. It embodies all of His wonderful traits. But Ephraim's and Judah's covenant love was like "a morning cloud" and the "dew" that quickly disappear before the rising face of the sun. What a powerful image to depict their superficial professions of loyalty!

Therefore (v. 5) shows that the constant turning of His people from Him caused God to take severe action to turn them back to Him and to teach them covenant love. God had *hewn* and *slain* Ephraim and Judah with His very own words (spoken through the prophets) calling into being His terrible chastisements. But *hewn* (v. 5),which means "cut to fashion," pictures God's judgment as both punitive and redemptive. God sent death and destruction to fashion His people according to His will.

God used His judgments upon Ephraim and Judah to teach them and others a lesson. The lesson taught, which was as clear as light going forth, is twofold. One, God "delights in loyalty rather than sacrifice and the knowledge of God more than burnt offerings," (v. 6). "The knowledge of God" is the intimate relationship with God that produces covenant love.

Two, *sacrifice* and *burnt offerings* were not ends in themselves. Rather they point to the shed blood of Christ by which believers' sins are forgiven and by which their life is totally offered up in consecrated service to God. When believers experience God personally in Christ and thus share His covenant love, they fulfill the true purpose for which God gave the sacrificial system.

The Israelites tended to assume that performing proper religious rituals was the heart of true religion. Hosea and other prophets insisted that outward religious observances should be expressions of, not substitutes for, knowing God and living for Him. This was one of several common themes of Hosea and the other eighth-century prophets. (See, for example, Isa. 1:10-17; Amos 5:21-24; Mic. 6:6-8.) Jesus also proclaimed the same message (see Matt. 15:1-14; 23:23).

The Gospels record two occasions when Jesus quoted Hosea 6:6. Each time Jesus was trying to help the Pharisees see that He, not they, was acting in accordance with the Scriptures. On one occasion, the Pharisees criticized Jesus for eating with sinners. Jesus referred to Hosea 6:6 in order to reinforce His words, "I did not come to call the righteous but sinners" (Matt. 9:13). On another occasion, the Pharisees accused Jesus' disciples of violating the Sabbath by eating grain as they passed through the grainfields. Jesus quoted Hosea 6:6 to challenge their rigid legalism (Matt. 12:7).

But (v. 7) contrasts what God desired of His people with what He found in them. Israel had deep-seated sin that kept them from God, prevented His healing them, and demanded His judging them. Hosea described their sins in terms of transgression of the covenant, treachery, wrongdoing, bloody deeds, assault, murder, crime, harlotry, and defilement (vv. 7-10).

The people of Judah also would experience terrible affliction to purge them from their sin (v. 11). In the end God would restore the fortunes of His people. Then all of God's people would know Him and show to Him and to one another covenant love.

Lessons for Life From Hosea 5:1—6:11

A Gallup poll reveals the same shallow consecration to God in America as was found in Israel during Hosea's day. According to Dr. George Gallup, Jr., Americans appear to be religious but do not practice what they say they believe. Less than 10 percent of Americans are deeply committed Christians. Moreover, according to Gallup, "the churched are just as likely as the unchurched to engage in unethical behavior."[1] Here are four facts to remember as we seek to use Hosea's message to bring America to God.

Moral decay is deadly.—Moral decay can destroy us, our families, and our nation just as it did ancient Israel unless we turn to God.

Superficial consecration to God is inadequate.—Going through the motions of being religious cannot substitute for true devotion to God. Being religious but lost is not confined to Israel of Hosea's day. Jesus said: "Not everyone who says to Me, 'Lord, Lord,' will enter the kingdom of heaven; but he who does the will of My Father who is in heaven" (Matt. 7:21). Those who continually practice sin show by their actions that they are not God's children (see Matt. 7:22-23).

Repentance involves turning to God from sin.—Anything that stops short of turning to God and turning from sin is not real repentance. Conviction of sin often leads to repentance, but conviction by itself is not repentance. Some people feel conviction but do not repent.

Genuine repentance brings renewal.—When we turn to God with all of our heart, God will give us new life in the same way that He promised to give new life to Israel. Then God will bless us, our families, and our nation.

---

1. Mark Wingfield, *The Baptist Message*, 6 June 1991, pp.1-2.

Personal Learning Activities

1. What did the Israelites' life of sin show? ____________
2. True ☐ False ☐ When God judged Israel for sin, Israel quickly repented and remained loyal to Him.
3. What three verbs did God use in His call to repentance?
   ____________ , ____________ , ____________
4. True ☐ False ☐ Repentance is turning from sin to God.
5. List three of the six reasons Israel would be punished.
   ____________ , ____________ , ____________
6. True ☐ False ☐ The background of Hosea 5:8 may be the civil war between Judah and Israel around 735 B.C.
7. True ☐ False ☐ Since Israel was so deep in sin, earnest seeking after God would not bring blessing.
8. Hosea compares Israel's loyalty to ____________ , denoting ____________ .
9. A Gallup poll revealed that less than ____% of Americans are deeply committed Christians.
10. When we sincerely turn to God, He will give us ____________ .

Answers: 1. they didn't know God personally. 2. false. 3. hear, give heed, listen. 4. false. 5. played the harlot, defiled herself, deeds prevented return to God, pride got in the way of asking for help, sought help from fertility gods, dealt treacherously against God. 6. true. 7. false. 8. a morning cloud, lack of permanence. 9. ten. 10. new life; blessings on ourselves, family, nation.

6

ISRAEL: A DECEITFUL PEOPLE

Hosea 7:1-16

How do you feel when someone lies to you? How does deception affect your dealings with people who have deceived you? Most of us feel hurt, angry, and frustrated by lies and deceit. We lose confidence and trust in those who deceive us. Such trust is the foundation for all human interaction—whether citizens' trust in governing officials, consumers' trust in merchants, employees' trust in employers, employers' trust in employees, friends' trust in friends, or family members' trust in other family members. When deceit replaces truth, the foundation for human interaction and relationships is eroded. Thus deceit destroys the foundation of government, business, friendship, and family.

The people of Hosea's day were a deceitful people. They dealt falsely with God and with one another. They professed loyalty to the Lord, but actually served heathen gods. Their kings and princes acted out of greed and self-interest to practice deceit and treachery. The deceit of the king and princes mirrored what was happening at all levels of society. For example, Hosea and Amos accused the merchants of that day of using various dishonest schemes to cheat the poor (Hos. 12:7; Amos 8:4-6).

As you study Hosea 7:1-16, look for evidences of deceit and related sins in ancient Israel. Also let God speak to you about the dangers of these same sins today.

Summary of 7:1-16

Hosea 7:1-16 concludes God's indictment of the Israelites for their sin, which began in 4:1. God continued to describe the Israelites' sin, guilt, and imminent destruction. Reference to their redemption occurs only in God's statement of His desire to heal (vv. 1, 13) and in His commitment to "chastise them in accordance with the proclamation" (v. 12).

The focus of 7:1-16 is upon Israel's deceitful heart which caused the people to "deal falsely" (v. 1) with God and men. Because of their deceitful hearts they defied God's healing (vv. 1-2); delighted in crime, adultery, debauchery, and anarchy (vv. 3-7); adopted heathen ways (vv. 8-10); turned from God to destructive allies (vv. 11-12), and rejected and devised evil against God (vv. 13-16). God in His redemptive love yearned to heal and restore the Israelites (vv. 1,13). In their enslavement to sin, however, they would not return or call upon Him (vv. 7,10,13-14,16). The result would be destruction for their nation and dispersion among the nations for survivors (vv. 13,16).

Defying Healing (7:1-2)

A dear friend has cancer. For two years his cancer has resisted every attempt at healing. New drugs brought new hope; each treatment has been followed by a fresh outbreak of the cancer. We continue to pray for healing.

The Israelites had terminal sin cancer. In contrast with our inability to cure cancer, God was able and willing to heal the cancer of sin. The Israelites were not willing to be healed. In fact, the people of Israel defied God's healing by sinning willfully. Hosea 7 continues the thought of 6:4-11, which describes the Israelites' moral corruption. What was God to do (6:4)? How could He bring healing when the people of Israel were unwilling to turn to Him? Even their cries to Him were expressions of corrupt hearts. The Israelites defiled God's holiness by identifying Him with fertility gods. The sacrifices involved immoral acts that offended God (6:6,10).

Heal is one of Hosea's words for redemption (v. 1; see also 5:13; 6:1). In its larger sense, healing involves full restoration to God with forgiveness (14:4). "When I would heal Israel" certainly expresses God's desire to bring healing to the Israelites of Hosea's day. The major emphasis, however, is upon God's past attempts to bring healing through prophetic rebuke. (6:5).

Each of God's attempts to heal Israel brought fresh outbreaks of sin. Ephraim and Samaria, respectively the dominant tribe and capital city of the Northern Kingdom, set the pace for Israel's moral corruption. Ephraim and Samaria were also responsible for the evil political decisions that led Israel from God to seek national salvation through changing kings and making alliances (vv. 7,11).

The last part of verse 1 points to the reason for the constant outbreak of sin in Israel. The Israelites' problem was their deceitful heart, which caused them to "deal falsely" with their God and their fellowman. The people dealt falsely with God and one another. They professed loyalty to God, but their actions showed that their loyalty was no more real or lasting than a morning mist (6:4). This kind of deceit against God bred deceitful dealings with others. The land became filled with thieves and bandits.

Some of the thieves were desperate people who resorted to breaking and entering someone's home or business for the purpose of stealing. Others were bandits who used force to plunder the goods of others. Still others were the people of power and influence who used their positions to enrich themselves by a policy of lies and deceit (7:3). If their society is anything like ours, the latter group was generally more successful in escaping disclosure or punishment by the law.

The most blatant result of their false dealing was that it desensitized and enslaved them to sin. They no longer considered in their hearts that God *remembers* (records and punishes) their sin (v. 2). "Now their deeds are all around them" means that their sins enslaved them like a prison wall. "They are before My face" means that they blatantly committed their sin before God without shame or fear of God's vengeance.

Delighting in Crime, Adultery, Debauchery, and Anarchy (7:3-7)

Verses 3-7 focus on the moral corruption of Israel's political leaders. The king and the high priest were God's two special representatives in the land. They were supposed to lead the nation to carry out its work as God's people. Simply stated, the high priest and his priestly associates were to teach the law of God. The king and his civil associates were to see that God's law was applied throughout the land. The king and the high priest were to be loyal servants of God and to provide godly examples for all people to follow. Jeroboam the son of Nebat (Jeroboam I), however, made Israel to sin by establishing the cult of the golden calf with its state-appointed priesthood (see 1 Kings 12:25-33). The state-appointed priests followed the king's leadership in pushing the fertility cults as the state religion (see Amos 7:10-13). Every king thereafter, including Jeroboam the son of Joash (Jeroboam II) in whose reign Hosea prophesied (1:1), walked in the evil ways of Jeroboam I.

Jeroboam II and his successors were so corrupt that they not only failed to punish wrongdoers but rejoiced in their crime. This seems to be the meaning of the words "with their wickedness they make the king glad" (v. 3). The king probably received lucrative "kickbacks" from them. The *princes*, the subordinate civil officials, also were parties to the greed and deceit. Notice the word *lies*. They, like the king, were happy with a system that used deceit to enrich themselves and further their own purposes.

Deceit and greed often go together. The old saying "money talks" continues to be as true as it ever was. If enough money is involved, many people are willing to go along with all kinds of evils.

The political leaders were also adulterers (v. 4). All those who made up the political leadership of the land (including the king, his wives, his sons, his daughters, his servants and his friends) were involved in promiscuously giving themselves to each other in these immoral acts. Their promiscuity was a deep-seated way of life, which was spawned by their licentious worship.

The analogy of the heated oven illustrates the intense nature of the political leaders' sin. Their passion for adultery resembled the baker's oven that was always kept heated and stoked to brighter flame when the dough was ready for baking. Their adulterous passions always burned in their hearts. They stoked these passions to red-hot intensity as opportunity for the act presented itself.

In terms of human relationships, adultery is the ultimate act

Israel's heated passion for idolatry was like an oven baking hot bread. "They are all adulterers like an oven heated by the baker." (7:4)

of deceit, betrayal, and treachery. Marriage is the one-flesh union of husband and wife. To be successful, marriage requires complete trust and absolute faithfulness. When a married person breaks that trust by unfaithfulness, the person breaks a sacred vow and betrays a loving spouse. Hosea knew the pain of this kind of deceit and betrayal. Unfortunately, so do many people today.

The king and his court were also guilty of debauchery (v. 5). "On the day of our king" may refer to the king's birthday or to his coronation day. Hosea cites two examples of their debauchery on such feast days. First, the princes would become sick with too much wine. Reference may be to the princes using wine to make the king sick and weak. "The princes have made him sick with bottles of wine" (KJV) may mean that the princes used alcoholic beverage to take away the king's sensitivity to their evil intent and to destroy his ability to resist them. (See 1 Kings 16:8-10 for an illustration of the use of alcohol to facilitate the assassination of a king.)

The second example of the royal court's debauchery is the king stretching "out his hand with scoffers" (v. 5). *Scoffers* (scorners) are those who turn away from God and mock Him and those whom He has set in authority. In his drunken stupor, the king opened his arms to these scoffers as trusted friends. Hosea and his contemporaries, Amos and Isaiah, were among the prophets whom the scoffers mocked.

The political leaders were also guilty of conspiracy (vv. 6-7). Hosea continued his hot-oven analogy (v. 4). This time he referred to conspirators who, with burning, deep-seated passion to usurp the throne of Israel, plotted and waited for the ideal moment to strike. Then, with red-hot intensity they would execute their heinous deed. "All of them are hot like an oven" shows how widespread was the spirit of rebellion. The result was anarchy.

Conspiracy was a way of life from the beginning for the Northern Kingdom. (See 1 Kings 14:20; 15:25-28.) Conspiracy intensified in the kingdom's last years. Of Israel's last six kings, only Menahem left the throne by natural death (see 2 Kings 15:22). Zechariah, Shallum, Pekahiah, and Pekah were assassinated. (See 2 Kings 15:8-10,13-14,22,25,30.) The king of Assyria dethroned and imprisoned Hoshea, Israel's last king, when he took Israel into captivity (see 2 Kings 17:4). Reference to these fallen kings probably means that Hosea's prophetic ministry extended somewhat past the reign of Jeroboam II. Many scholars see Hosea's ministry as lasting even unto the disintegration of the Northern Kingdom in 722 B.C.

When political, social, and economic problems become so desperate that anarchy results, people sometimes turn to God. But in Israel God said, "None of them calls on me" (v. 7). The people and rulers did not consult God concerning whom they should place on Israel's throne. Neither did the people or the rulers call upon Him in the distress of their anarchy. All sought to promote their own agenda. In wicked self-determination, they totally separated themselves from their God.

Adopting Heathen Ways (7:8-10)

One morning I turned to a few chores and neglected the oatmeal I had put on to cook. When I remembered and rushed to the kitchen, I found the oatmeal burned on the bottom, raw on top, and unfit to eat.

Hosea spoke of Israel as "a cake not turned" (v. 8). *Cake* refers to a small piece of barley bread that was cooked on flat stones. It was much like our pancakes. *Not turned* means that it was burned on one side and raw on the other. Hosea probably referred to Israel's uselessness as the result of their half-baked consecration to God. The people were set in their half-baked condition and, thus, fit only to be thrown out.

A basic problem of Israel is expressed by the words, "Ephraim mixes himself with the nations" (v. 8). Israel was a holy nation because of the covenant with God (see Ex. 19:6). Among other things, a "holy nation" meant that Israel was to keep itself separated from other nations and consecrated to God for His redemptive purposes. God in turn would protect and provide for Israel as His treasured possession (see Ex. 19:5). The Israelites were thrown into contact with people of other nations, particularly after they entered Canaan. Their pagan neighbors did not worship the Lord or feel bound by the moral expectations of the holy God. Instead they worshiped gods through practices considered immoral and corrupt by God. Throughout Israel's history, the people were tempted to forsake the Lord and His high expectations and to adopt the corrupt practices of their pagan neighbors. (See 1 Sam. 8:5; 1 Kings 16:31.) This compromise with pagan practices finally destroyed Israel as a nation.

The *strangers* (v. 9) who consumed Israel's strength were probably more than non-Israelites. Reference is to those who were loathsome because of their idolatrous practices. The Israelites could have been kept perpetually young and strong by maintaining their consecration to God. In adopting pagan ways, the Israelites corrupted themselves until they were like a weak old man tottering toward the grave.

This expression, "yet he does not know it" (v. 9), is repeated for emphasis. The purpose of the repetition is to magnify the hardening, blinding, and damning effects of sin. The people of Israel brought themselves to a moral state in which they were ignorant and insensitive to their corruption and weakness. They willfully and persistently rejected God and gave themselves to the idolatrous practices of their pagan neighbors.

God continued to reach out to the Israelites, but in pride they refused to return to Him (v. 10). As in 5:5, "the pride of Israel" may refer to God. However, reference seems to be to Israel's arrogance. "For all this" (v. 10) summaries the various ways, including chastisement, by which God called Israel to return to Him (see Amos 3:6-13). Israel answered with a resounding "No!" In their blind arrogance they would seek personal and national salvation through their own efforts.

Turning From God to Destructive Allies (7:11-12)

A pigeon wandered into our church sanctuary and could not find its way out. In its disorientation, the pigeon flew around for days seeking a way out. Finally death came. The pigeon could have saved itself if only it had flown to me or one of the others seeking its rescue. In our rescue attempts we unsuccessfully used a net.

Israel became disoriented "like a silly dove, without sense" (v. 11) as the result of turning from God to embrace the practices of pagan neighbors. Comparing Israel to a "silly dove" means that Israel was easily enticed and deceived.

Egypt and Assyria dominated the international scene during Hosea's day.Whether Israel called to Egypt or went unto Assyria for help depended upon the circumstances. King Menahem of Israel paid Pul, the king of Assyria (also known as Tiglath-pileser), a thousand talents of silver to confirm for himself Israel's throne (see 2 Kings 15:19,29). King Pekah of Israel joined with King Rezin of Syria to oppose Assyria's takeover (see 2 Kings 15:37; Isa. 7:1). They doubtlessly looked to Egypt for help. They also besieged Jerusalem to force Judah to join them, but Judah turned to Assyria (see 2 Kings 16:5-8; Isa. 7:1-11). Hoshea, Israel's last king, sought to secure his throne by alliance with Assyria, but then turned to Egypt in rebellion against Assyria. The king of Assyria swept him and Israel away for looking to Egypt. (See 2 Kings 17:3-6.)

God pictured Himself standing with a net in His hand to snare "dove" Israel in her to-and-fro flight between Egypt and Assyria. Whether the capture is good or bad for the birds depends on the captor's purpose. In the case of the pigeon in our sanctuary, our purpose in seeking its capture was to release the pigeon to the outside. God's purpose in capturing Israel was to "chastise them in accordance with the proclamation" (v. 12). *Chastise* means "to teach through judgment."

The proclamation refers to Moses setting forth to the assembled Israelites God's conditions for blessings and warnings of chastisement for disobedience (see Lev. 26:1-46; Deut. 27:11—30:20). The chastisement would be in degrees but would finally encompass desolation of the land and dispersion of the people among the nations. God's purpose was redemptive. He would destroy the ungodly but purify the repentant (Lev. 26:40-45). The final result would be a redeemed remnant in the land experiencing God's promised blessings.

Rejecting and Devising Evil Against God (7:13-16)

Desolating judgment was imminent for Israel. *Woe* (v. 13) was spoken upon those who were doomed or dead. It was not a call to repentance but a sorrowful warning of the inevitable consequences of sin.

"I would redeem them" (v. 13) is literally, "I would ransom them." The larger idea of ransom is to redeem by paying the price. God was willing to pay the price to redeem the Israelites, but they were not yet willing for Him to redeem them. In verses 13-16 God cited seven reasons for their coming destruction.

The first is that Israel was now set in rebellion (v. 13). The verbs *strayed* and *rebelled* depict the Israelites fixed in their rebellious departure from the Lord.

Second, Israel was set in false witness against the Lord (v. 13). What lies did the Israelites speak against the Lord? Perhaps they voiced their conviction that the Lord God of Israel, as preached by Hosea and other true prophets, could not save them in their complex world. More likely the lies refer to their saying that the Lord God of Israel was like the fertility gods.

The third reason for Israel's coming destruction was their insincerity in calling upon God (v. 14). The Israelites did not call to the Lord "from their heart." "Wail on their beds" may point to frantic acts in an effort to energize the fertility gods on their behalf (2:8-9) or to the despair because of the distress that had come upon them.

Fourth, the Israelites committed apostasy in the way they sought for grain and new wine (v. 14). God sent drought and marauding enemies to turn Israel back to Him. In their desperation for grain and new wine, the people cried to Him as their God (8:2). Their rituals, however, showed that they tried to manipulate Him as they would a fertility god.

The fifth reason for Israel's coming destruction was because the people "devised evil" against the Lord (v. 15). They betrayed God who had redeemed and nurtured them. The evil that they devised against the Lord was leading the nation away from Him instead of to Him.

Sixth, the Israelites did not seek God (v. 16). "They turn, but not upward" is another picture of their disorientation. They turned around and around looking for solutions to their problems. In their stupidity they never looked upward to Him who was willing and able to heal. Because they had turned from God and involved themselves in the practices of their pagan neighbors, the Israelites were as useless to God as "a deceitful bow" is to a warrior or a hunter. Furthermore, their compromising could no more lead to their goals of peace and prosperity than they could hit a target with "a deceitful bow."

The seventh reason for which God would send desolation was the scornful speaking by Israel's princes (v. 16). The princes would die by the sword because their insolent speech expressed a scoffing heart. "Derision in the land of Egypt" probably refers to the new bondage into which Israel would go for rejecting God and devising evil against Him.

Verses 13-16 further emphasize the theme of a deceitful people found throughout chapter 7. The people spoke lies against God. Although they outwardly professed loyalty to God, they served other gods. Such evil actually amounted to the same thing as devising evil against God. As a result, Israel was like a deceitful bow, which is useless for its intended purpose. No wonder God sadly announced that such a deceitful nation is doomed.

Lessons For Life From Hosea 7:1-16

As we study Hosea 7:1-16, the parallels between ancient Israel and modern America are all too obvious:

Deceit destroys the fabric of a society.—When people deal falsely with God, they also deal falsely with other people. When deceit replaces integrity in the lives of enough people, society is doomed.

Greed and deceit often go together.—When enough money is involved, people are tempted to do whatever is necessary to further their own interests. Such people often bend the truth if lying helps them get what they want.

Political deceit mirrors a society that has replaced integrity with self-interest.—People in public life face many temptations to use their power and influence in ways that enrich them or further their own self-interest. Hosea 7:3 reminds us that this is nothing new. Representatives from government are by no means immune to this ancient sin of kings and princes. How often in our own lifetimes have elected officials adopted deceit as a normal operating procedure? Public policy mirrors private practice. Before average citizens try to put all the blame on the politicians, they need to recognize how pervasive greed and deceit have become throughout all layers of society.

Adultery is the ultimate expression of deceit in human relations.—Who can hurt us the most? Enemies hurt us, but we expect enemies to hurt us. We do not expect friends and loved ones to hurt us; therefore, betrayal by a friend or loved one hurts more than the wounds caused by enemies. Nothing hurts so much as the betrayal of life's most sacred bond—the one-flesh union of marriage. Adultery is the ultimate expression of deceit in human relations because it betrays the trust and love of a spouse and breaks a vow of faithfulness made in the presence of God and society.

Christians in every generation are tempted to adopt the ideas and practices of non-Christian society.—Throughout Israel's history, a basic problem was the people's infatuation with the heathen ways of people who did not know God. The Israelites yielded to the temptation to compromise their distinctive faith and life-style by turning to other gods and adopting their immoral ways. People of faith in every generation face the same basic temptation. American Christians are not tempted to worship Baal, but we are tempted to compromise our commitment and way of life by adopting the ideas and standards of a non-Christian society. The New Testament uses Old Testament language to challenge Christians to dare to live out our commitment to Christ in daily living (1 Pet. 1:13-16).

Personal Learning Activities

1. True ☐ False ☐ God was willing to restore Israel, but Israel was not willing to be healed.
2. The constant outbreak of sin in Israel was due to the people's deceitful ______________________.
3. True ☐ False ☐ The Israelites committed sin, but at least they expressed shame and displayed fear of God.
4. God's two special representatives in the land were the ______________ and the ______________.
5. List the two examples of debauchery mentioned in Hosea. ______________, ______________
6. The hot-oven analogy was used to illustrate what sins? ______________, ______________
7. "Mixes with the other nations" means ______________ ______________________.
8. God was to "capture" the Israelites in order to ________ them.
9. *Woe* is a ______________________.
10. List one truth you learned from this chapter. ______________________

Answers: 1. true. 2. heart. 3. false. 4. king, high priest. 5. princes became sick with too much wine, king trusted scoffers. 6. the passion for adultery, conspiracy to usurp the throne. 7. adopting pagan practices of one's neighbors. 8. chastise. 9. solemn warning of the inevitable consequences of sin. 10. personal answer.

7

Reap the Whirlwind!

Hosea 8:1-14

My family and I were in Hurricane Camille, which brought destruction and death in 1969 to the Mississippi Gulf Coast. Two hundred and twenty people died, some because they failed to heed the warning of coming destruction. A few even had "hurricane parties." They stayed in their beach apartments and houses to celebrate their lack of respect for nature's wrath. The wind and waves swept those people away.

Carried by tornadic winds, water flooded into our home on Sunday, August 17, at midnight. Betty and I, along with our two daughters Kathy and Angela, were trapped inside our home. We were helpless as the water covered the first and second floors of our split-level home and moved up the stairs where we were huddled together. The tornadic winds prevented our escape to the roof. We called frantically for help as the waters continued to come up the stairs, but we could not get an answer. When we finally reached an emergency telephone, no one could help us. We experienced great material loss, but we thanked God for saving our lives. Our hearts still bleed for those who lost personal possessions and their lives as well.

Summary of Hosea 8:1-14

I do not know why Hurricane Camille struck the Mississippi Gulf Coast. Neither do I know why some were spared while others met their death. God, however, told us why He destroyed Israel of Hosea's day.

Israel had sown to the wind. Now they would reap the whirlwind (8:7). The harvest law is threefold. We reap what we sow; we reap later than we sow; and we reap more than we sow. For many years Israel acted in rebellion and deceit against the

Lord their God. Specifically, they established their nation in rebellion against the God-appointed throne of David. To maintain their political independence, they claimed to worship the Lord God of Israel under the figure of golden calves with their own priesthood and places of worship. They pulled to their bosom the spirit of harlotry by giving themselves to the licentious practices of calf worship. Now the whirlwinds of destruction would blow them away.

Hosea 8:1-14 is part of the larger section 8:1—10:15 which contains the third of the four strong themes in the Book of Hosea. Hosea 1:1—3:5 stresses God's faithful love for unfaithful Israel. Hosea 4:1—7:16 shows God's indictment of Israel's many sins. Hosea 8:1—10:15 warns of the sure judgment that comes to those who stubbornly reject God's love and continue in their sins.

God continued in 8:1-14 to point to the sin for which He would judge the Israelites. The focus shifts to the judgment that would desolate their land and sweep them into captivity. In keeping with the theme of sowing and reaping, Israel would now reap the harvest of rejecting God (vv. 1-3), the harvest of self-will (vv. 4-7), the harvest of embracing pagan allies and their ways (vv. 8-10), the harvest of licentious worship (vv. 11-13), and the harvest of forgetting God (v. 14).

Harvest of Rejecting God (8:1-3)

Judgment is coming upon America for rejecting God as it came upon Israel of Hosea's day. The role of God's people is to warn the citizenry of the coming destruction (see Ezek. 33:1-6).

Verses 1-3 are God's command to Hosea the prophet to warn the Israelites of their imminent destruction because they had rejected God. An enemy would swoop down on them because they had rejected God's covenant and broken His laws (v. 1). God told Hosea that the people would claim to know God to avert destruction (v. 2). Because they confessed Him with their lips but rejected God and good, He would exact His judgment through Israel's enemy (v. 3).

Warning of Imminent Destruction (v. 1)

Trumpet (v. 1) refers to the ram's horn. The blast of the trumpet carried the highest authority and demanded immediate obedience. It was used to warn of the approaching enemy (see Ezek. 33:3-4). God sent prophets like Amos and Hosea to sound the trumpet in Israel. The warning was to stimulate the people to repentance. Israel could no longer save itself as a nation; individual Israelites could still save themselves by turning to God from their sin.

The judgment coming in Israel is described as an enemy who is like an eagle. The term *eagle* here includes both the eagle and the vulture. It is used to describe the fierce invader that God promised through Moses to bring on the people of Israel if they turned from Him (see Deut. 28:49). As such, *eagle* is used of the Assyrian and Babylonian invaders (see Jer. 4:13; Hab. 1:8). God commanded Hosea to sound the trumpet because this terrible bird of prey was settling on the land to devour it. The reason for this terrible judgment is explained in the last part of verse 1. The people of Israel had transgressed God's covenant and rebelled against His law.

God took the initiative in offering a covenant to Israel at Mount Sinai. Based on God's redemptive love for Israel, God called them into a special relationship with Him (Ex. 19:4-6). The special relationship involved wholehearted devotion to God to be expressed in obedience to God. The law, especially the Ten Commandments, spelled out the requirements of Israel's covenant with God. The Ten Commandments provided abiding principles for Israel to live in relation to God and to man. The rest of the Law provided applications of these principles to certain areas of life.

On the plain of Moab, God ratified this covenant with the Israelites through Moses. He added blessings for obedience and curses for disobedience to the covenant (see Deut. 27:9-10; 28:1-2,15). Among these curses was the promise to bring on disobedient Israel the terrible "nation. . . as the eagle swoops down" (Deut. 28:49). In Hosea 8:1, the prophet announced the coming of the eagle judgment on Israel for rejecting the covenant relationship with God as evidenced in Israel's continually breaking God's laws.

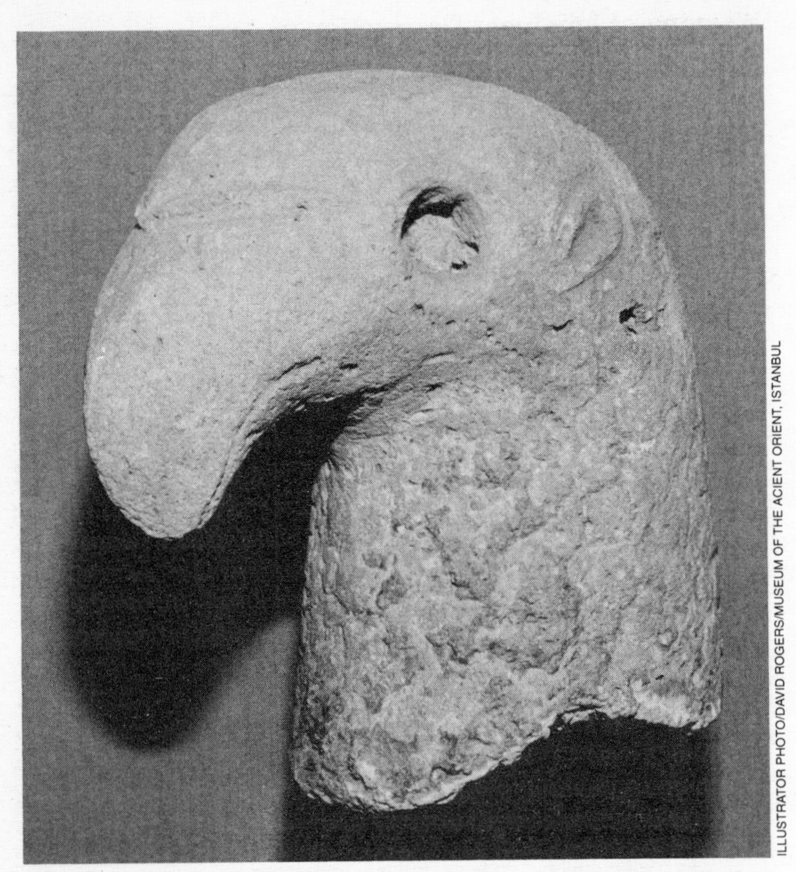
ILLUSTRATOR PHOTO/DAVID ROGERS/MUSEUM OF THE ACIENT ORIENT, ISTANBUL

The swift flight of an eagle pictured the rapidly approaching Assyrian army. "Like an eagle the enemy comes against the house of the Lord." (8:1)

When the *eagle* pounced on Israel, the people would cry in horror for God's help. "My God, we of Israel know Thee" (v. 2) was the Israelites' claim to have a personal relationship with God. Their words would have been an appropriate prayer for people in covenant relation with God. The problem was that their outward profession and prayer did not match reality.

God replied to Israel's prayer that Israel had "rejected the good" (v. 3). This is another way of saying that they had rejected the covenant relation with God by breaking God's laws. The word *good* stresses that by rejecting God and His laws, Israel rejected the good life of abundant blessings that God wanted to give them.

Good especially refers to the way of life prescribed by God for Israel in keeping the covenant. It refers to Moses' declaration in the plain of Moab that he set before Israel in the covenant "life and good" (Deut. 30:15, KJV). Rejection of the covenant would bring "death and adversity" (Deut. 30:15).

One of the deceptions of Satan is that God and His Word will rob people of the good life. The devil effectively used this temptation to deceive Adam and Eve into distrusting God's good intention for them. They forgot all the good that God offered to them and became preoccupied with the one prohibition. They accepted the lie that God's warning about the forbidden fruit was intended to deny to them the truly good life. Since this temptation worked so well, the devil has continued to use it.

The Israelites were like sinners in every generation. They rejected God and His ways in order to find the good life on their own terms. The tragedy is that those who reject God also reject good and find death instead.

Harvest of Self-Will (8:4-7)

Israel rebelled against God in two specific ways. The first was in setting up their kingdom and kings in neglect and opposition to God (v. 4a). The second was in establishing their own worship of God around the golden calves in violation of God's law (vv. 4b-6). As a result of making their own kings and making their own gods, Israel made their own judgment (v. 7).

Illegitimate Kingdom and Kings (v. 4a)

Jeroboam the son of Nebat (Jeroboam I) established the Northern Kingdom (Israel) in opposition to the God-appointed throne of David. In the breaking away of the ten northern tribes under Jeroboam I, the house of David reaped the result of Solomon's following other gods (see 1 Kings 11:9-13). The division of the kingdom was not to be permanent but to chastise the house of David (see 1 Kings 11:39).

God in turn offered to establish Jeroboam I and his seed on the throne of the Northern Kingdom for the duration of the chastisement if Jeroboam would walk in God's way as David walked (see 1 Kings 11:35-39). Jeroboam I refused God's offer and set up calf worship in the name of the Lord God of Israel to maintain his political independence from the Southern Kingdom (see 1 Kings 12:25-33). Every king of Israel after Jeroboam I followed him in the path of calf worship.

This was the history behind God's words: "They have set up kings, but not by Me." Self-will characterized all that Israel did in relation to their kingdom and royal officials (kings and princes). "Not by Me" as well as "I did not know it" mean that God did not acknowledge or approve their kings.

Illegitimate Worship (vv. 4b-6)

Idols also were an expression of Israel's self-will. God forbade idol-making (see Ex. 20:3-6). Idolatry was a capital offense in Israel (see Lev. 20:3; Ezek. 14:7). The idolater has no part in God's kingdom (see 1 Cor. 6:9). Therefore, to make and worship idols brought destruction.

The focus of verses 5-7 is upon golden calf worship for which God warned He would cut Israel off. The two calves, which Jeroboam I set up in high places in Dan to the north and in Bethel to the south (see 1 Kings 12:29), were similar to the golden calf made by Aaron in the wilderness (see Ex. 32:4). The calves were probably made of wood and overlaid with gold since they could be burned, splintered, and ground into powder (see Ex. 32:20; Hos. 8:6).

Jeroboam I probably meant the calves to be a substitute for the ark of God in Jerusalem as the throne of the invisible God. However, his words, "Behold your gods, O Israel, that brought you up from the land of Egypt" (1 Kings 12:28) suggest that he made the calves as images of God Himself. The people who made the golden calf at Sinai said much the same thing (Ex. 32:4). Thus, the calves identified the Lord God of Israel with the fertility gods worshiped throughout the ancient Near East. God's response to golden calves in Hosea's day was the same as in Moses' day (see Ex. 32:10). God said, "My anger burns against them!" (v. 5). As part of God's judgment, Moses made the people drink the burned and ground golden calf (mixed with water) to symbolize that they would reap the horrible results of calf worship (see Ex. 32:20).

God's anger is the measured response of His holiness to sin. In love and faithfulness to His covenant promises, God is slow to anger and plenteous in mercy (see Ex. 34:6-7). God's anger had been building against Israel for over two hundred years because of calf worship. The cup of the Israelites' sin now stood full and overflowing, and God in His anger would sweep them away. He would bring an end to their national life by the Assyrian captivity. Their willful, persistent practice of calf worship reflected the depth of their sin. Since the calf was hand-made and could be broken into pieces, it was not God (v. 6). God's judgment would purify His people from calf worship and return them to right living.

Reaping the Whirlwind (v. 7)

The first part of verse 7 explains the reason for Israel's destruction and the second part, typified by empty grain heads, pictures the vanity of fertility worship. Because they had "sowed the wind," they would "reap the whirlwind." *Whirlwind* refers to devastating storm winds. Rejecting God and good (vv. 1-3) and embracing the winds of harlotry and false kings (vv. 4-6), the people of Israel sowed the winds of their destruction. Their wicked deeds multiplied and intensified across the years like a tropical storm builds into hurricane intensity. Now these hurricane winds would destroy the nation.

Certain conditions in nature result in tornadoes or hurricanes. Certain sinful actions result in a whirlwind of judgment. The words *sow* and *reap* remind us of Galatians 6:7: "Do not be deceived, God is not mocked; for whatever a man sows, this he will also reap." Those who sow and nurture the seeds of sin eventually will reap the harvest of sin. Because time usually elapses between sowing and reaping, some people feel that they will never be called to account for their sins. Such an attempt to mock God is foolish. The harvest will surely come to those who sow the seeds of sin.

Harvest of Embracing Pagan Allies and Their Ways (8:8-10)

Israel and Assyria remind us of the hunter and the bear who negotiated to the hurt of the hunter but to the delight of the bear. Before the hunter shot the bear with his carefully aimed rifle, the bear suggested that they work together to help each get what each wanted. After the negotiation the bear walked away alone. Each had his desire—the bear a full stomach and the man a fur coat.

The Assyrians gobbled up Galilee and Gilead in the invasion of 733 B.C. Samaria along with the whole nation fell in 722 B.C. God chose Israel from among the nations to be His peculiar treasure (see Ex. 19:5, KJV). In their desire to be like other nations and to find security among the nations, the people of Israel adopted the ways of their pagan neighbors and entered into alliances with them (see 7:8; 9:1). Israel was enslaved among the nations as a useless vessel, possessing nothing desirable or precious (v. 8).

"For they have gone up to Assyria" (v. 9) tells why Israel was devoured. In going up to Assyria, Israel was "like a wild donkey all alone." This analogy points to Israel's obstinacy. Jeremiah compared Israel to a "wild donkey" that "sniffs the wind in her passion" and then moves headstrong for the desired lover (see Jer. 2:24).

The Israelites committed religious harlotry in turning from God to follow after the fertility gods. They committed political harlotry in turning from God to seek security among the nations. Harlotry, whether physical, religious, or political, always degrades. As a harlot Israel was no longer desirable. She must now pay to have lovers.

God warned that He would "gather them up" (v. 10). He would put a stop to their political as well as religious harlotry. God would take away whatever security they experienced through political harlotry and would judge them according to His purposes.

The expression "begin to diminish" suggests hardship and suffering. "The king of princes" may be a title for Tiglath-pileser, king of Assyria. According to this interpretation the diminishing would come from the heavy hand of Assyria's king. Another translation is: "And they shall cease for a little while from anointing king and princes" (v. 10, RSV[1]). According to this interpretation Israel would now begin to be without "king or prince" (3:4). How long is "a little while"? This indefinite period of judgment would be long enough for self-willed Israel to learn to live joyfully under the King whom God would give to them (3:5).

Harvest of Licentious Worship (8:11-13)

A bird-watcher observed an American eagle swoop down, clutch its prey, and begin to soar again into the heavens. As the bird-watcher continued to observe, he saw the American eagle stagger and then plummet to the ground. As quickly as possible he moved to the fallen eagle. He discovered that the eagle had pulled a badger feet first to its bosom and that the badger clawed out the eagle's heart.

How does Israel's sin of following fertility gods apply to modern America? Americans do not build golden calves and worship them. Like ancient Israel, however, Americans have embraced sexual sin, and it is clawing out America's heart.[2]

God said, "Ephraim has multiplied altars for sin" (v. 11). Multiplying altars was sin in itself, for the one and only acceptable altar for sacrifice was at Jerusalem (see Deut. 12:1-14; 1 Chron. 22:1). The "altars for sin" were fertility shrines. These altars led them deeper into sin.

One tragic result of their idolatry was concluding God's laws (the ones regulating true worship and godly living) to be foreign and loathsome. "Though I wrote for him ten thousand precepts of My law" (v. 12) means that God made known His will in many different ways. In spite of this, the people regarded God and His laws as strange and foreign.

God's "sacrificial gifts" refer to peace offerings (v. 13). These offerings involved joining God and other worshipers in a fellowship meal based on blood sacrifice (see Ex. 24:5-11). The blood, fat, kidneys, and liver of the sacrificial animals were offered on the altar to God as His part of the meal (see Lev. 3:1-5). The worshipers and the priests ate the rest of the sacrifice in the presence of the Lord (see Lev. 7:11-34). The peace offering denoted the oneness of God with His people and their oneness with Him and one another. In their spiritual blindness the Israelites assumed that mere engagement in the sacrificial ritual established oneness with God. God was not pleased with ritual apart from obedience to His laws concerning true worship (6:6).

God said He would "remember their iniquity" (v. 13). To *remember* means "to call to mind to punish." As a result of remembering their sin, God said they would "return to Egypt" (v. 13). This means to return to the kind of bondage Israel knew in Egypt. It does not mean bondage again in Egypt, but Egyptian-like bondage in Assyria (9:3; 11:5).

The word *remember* in Hosea 8:13 is the same word used in Jeremiah 31:34 to describe God's willingness to "remember" sin "no more." Jeremiah was speaking of the gracious provision of forgiveness under the new covenant. God has always been willing and able to forgive and forget sin when people truly repent and turn to Him in trust (Ex. 34:6-7; Ps. 103: 11-13; Isa. 1:18; 55:6-7; Mic. 7:18-19). The new covenant makes this abundantly plain through the death of Jesus Christ for sin and the proclamation of salvation by grace through faith.

The clear message of the Bible is that God yearns to be able to forgive sins and grant new life. However, equally clear is that stubborn refusal of God's love leads inevitably to reaping the harvest that has been sown. Sinners are condemned when they stubbornly persist in their sins and ignore God's calls to repentance.

Harvest of Forgetting God (8:14)

God cited here the basic reason for Israel being swallowed up. Forgetting God was Israel's root sin. The verb form of God as *Maker* pictures God making the Israelites His covenant people and continuously working through them to fulfill His redemptive purposes. The basic idea of *forgetting* seems to be "to leave something or someone from forgetfulness." The opposite of forgetting is remembering. In spite of Moses' warning not to forget God, the Israelites forgot to teach their children how and why God chose and redeemed them (see Deut. 4:9).

They forgot to fear, worship, and serve God and Him only (see Deut. 6:10-13). They forgot to praise God for His blessings and use those blessings for God's glory (see Deut. 8:11,17). They forgot that God would judge them for their sin (see Deut. 9:1,4). They forgot that God would fulfill His promises to them even if that required chastising them in order to redeem them (see Deut. 9:5,7).

God underscored two activities resulting from Israel's forgetting Him. In these activities He indicted Judah as well as Israel. The first was building *palaces* and the second was multiplying *fortified cities.* God probably meant the strongholds in which they trusted and the great houses that the rich built by gobbling up the poor. (See Amos 6:1-14.)

Lessons for Life from Hosea 8:1-14

When weather conditions are threatening, weather forecasters issue storm warnings. The Bible in general and Hosea 8:1-14 in particular contain a warning of a much more deadly storm than any tornado or hurricane. This warning contains several lessons for life.

Forgetting God must be easy; so many people do it.—It often begins with the failure to thank God for His goodness. This leads to a false sense of self-sufficiency as if we have outgrown any need of God. Other values and priorities replace the values and priorities of God's Word. Those who forget God drift into sins of all kinds.

Many people are confused about the good life.—The Bible says that God wants to give people what is good for them, but the devil tempts them to believe that God intends to deny them a life of real happiness and fulfillment. As a result, people turn from God and His way. By doing so, they think they will find the good life, but all they find is sin and death.

Sinners reap what they sow.—Seed that is sown eventually results in a harvest of what grows from that seed. An interval of time intervenes between sowing and reaping, but the harvest eventually comes. This agricultural law has a comparable moral and spiritual law. This law of sin and retribution is as sure as the law of the harvest. It grows out of the fact that God made us free and, therefore, morally accountable for what we do. Some people think they can continue to sow the seeds of sin but never reap the harvest of death. But they are wrong.

Sinners are condemned when they harden their hearts and spurn God's calls to repentance.—God in His mercy offers forgiveness and life through Jesus Christ, who died for our sins. Those who repent and believe are saved from sin, but those who reject God's salvation condemn themselves (John 3:16-21).

---

1. Scripture quotations marked (RSV) are from the *Revised Standard Version of the Bible*, copyright 1946, 1952, © 1971, 1973.
2. Roy T. Edgemon, *The Doctrines Baptists Believe* (Nashville: Convention Press, 1988), 43.

Personal Learning Activities

1. Israel had sown to the ______________ . Now Israel would reap the ______________________________ .
2. Hosea 8:1—10:15 focuses on the results of Israel's ______________________________ .
3. The ______________ served as a stimulus for repentance.
4. Israel's enemy was to swoop down like an ______________ .
5. Why was God going to destroy the people (8:1)? ______________________________
6. List the two ways Israel rebelled against God (8:4-7). ______________________________ ______________________________
7. The empty grain heads indicated ______________________ .
8. Israel fell to Assyria in the year ______________________ .
9. True ☐ False ☐ Oneness with God could be established by merely engaging in the sacrificial ritual.
10. Israel forgot four things. What were they? ______________________________ ______________________________ ______________________________ ______________________________

Answers: 1. wind, whirlwind. 2. unfaithfulness. 3. trumpet. 4. eagle. 5. they transgressed God's covenant and rebelled against God's law. 6. set up a kingdom and kings in opposition to God; established worship around calves. 7. the vanity of fertility worship. 8. 722 B.C. 9. false. 10. to fear, worship, and serve God alone; to praise God for His blessings and use them for His glory; that God would judge them for sin; that God would fulfill His promises even if chastisement was needed for redemption.

8

Time To Seek The Lord

Hosea 9:1—10:15

Herschel Ford told of the man who committed suicide by cutting himself loose from his ascending hot-air balloon. As the man ascended into the heavens, the people saw him cut one of the three ropes holding the passenger basket to the balloon. Then, in spite of their warning shouts, he cut the second rope. "Don't cut the last rope," they pled; but he cut the third rope and plunged to his death.[1]

For years the people of Israel cut the cords of love binding them to their God. In 9:1—10:15 we see them cut the last cord and plunge to their destruction as a nation.

The psalmist said, "Blessed is the nation whose God is the Lord" (Ps. 33:12). Similarly, Solomon wrote, "Righteousness exalts a nation, but sin is a disgrace to any people" (Prov. 14:34). Many nations, however, prefer the way of sin. The Old Testament prophets often confronted Israel as well as the Gentile nations with warnings of national calamity because of God's judgment for sins. A nation's failure to heed the promises and warnings of the prophets' messages led inevitably to destruction. The actions of the Israelites of Hosea's day are a lesson on how to commit national suicide (see Deut. 28:37).

Summary of 9:1—10:15

The time frame of 9:1—10:15 seems to be the reign of Hoshea, the son of Elah, Israel's last king (see 2 Kings 17:1-6). Israel's destruction had begun (9:7). If the people repented, they would experience forgiveness and a new beginning (10:12). The Israelites, however, refused God's call to repentance and plunged to their death (10:13-15). As seen in the double outline of the four sections in Hosea 9:1—10:15, Hosea continued his double emphasis on Israel's sins and the inevitable judgment on sin. Because of Israel's depravity, judgment had come (9:1-9). Because of Israel's persistent rebellion, judgment would sweep them away (9:10-17). Because of Israel's divided heart, their most cherished institutions would be destroyed (10:1-11). Because Israel refused to repent, the nation would be destroyed by devastating war (10:12-15).

Israel's Depravity: Judgment Has Come (9:1-9)

The first part of verse 7 sets the tone for verses 1-9. The prophet announced that the days of punishment and retribution had come. If the time frame of Hosea 9:1—10:15 is the final days of Israel, the Assyrians had already captured portions of Israel and carried many people into captivity (2 Kings 15:29). Hosea may have had in mind this beginning of the end when he wrote, "The days of punishment have come" (Hos. 9:7). Hosea spoke of judgment as an accomplished fact. What had already happened was only the beginning of the end; the end was sure to follow.

The Bible often speaks of judgment for persistent sin as if it were an accomplished fact. This is because the process of judgment is inherent in the sin itself. "The wages of sin is death" (Rom. 6:23) because sin results in spiritual death, and leads to the death of eternal separation from God.

Hosea declared that judgment had come because of the spiritual harlotry of the people (9:1-6), because they rejected God's word through His prophet (9:7-8), and because they sank ever deeper into depravity (9:9).

Judgment for Spiritual Harlotry (vv. 1-6)

Hosea 9:1 seems to indicate that the prophet had burst in on one of the Israelites' pagan celebrations. Hosea interrupted the Israelites' wild harvest celebration to announce that God would end their festival joy. Hosea condemned the Israelites' adoption of the fertility worship practices of their pagan neighbors. He commanded them to stop rejoicing "with exultation like the nations" (v. 1a), told them why God would make an end to their festival joy (v. 1b), and then explained what would occur for Israel under God's judgment (vv. 2-6).

Verse 1 is a concise summons of a theme not only of Hosea but also of much of the Old Testament. Hosea's distinctive emphasis was how God helped Hosea gain insight into Israel's sin as a result of Hosea's unhappy experience with Gomer. The Israelites forsook God and committed harlotry against God both figuratively and literally. They were spiritually unfaithful by turning to the Baals. Part of Baal worship involved sexual immorality.

Notice the words "like the nations." God had called Israel to be His distinctive people. Two things were to testify to their basic distinctiveness: (1) their wholehearted faith in the one true God and (2) their distinctive way of life based on the nature of God and revealed in His commandments. But as we have seen in passages like Hosea 7:8, the persistent temptation for Israel was to be "like the nations." Over and over in Israel's history the people compromised their distinctive faith and way of life. Baal worship was the most striking evidence of Israel's unfaithfulness to God.

Hosea underscored in verses 2-6 seven features of God's judgment upon the Israelites. One, He would strike at the heart of fertility worship by taking away the bountiful harvest (v. 2). Two, God would remove them from His land (v. 3). Three, He would place them in Assyria in Egyptian-like captivity (v. 3). Indeed, many Israelites had already been deported to Assyria (see 2 Kings 15:29). Four, God would bring an end to their wicked worship (v. 4). Five, God would cut them off from the appointed feast days (vv. 5-6a). Six, they would die in captivity (v. 6). Seven, God would desolate Israel's fertility idols and shrines (v. 6).

Memphis (v. 6) is the site of Egypt's great burial grounds. Those who escaped to Egypt to avoid the Assyrian takeover would meet death there. To write that "Memphis will bury them," was like saying Israel was headed for the cemetery. I have a piece of marble from Memphis. It reminds me of the death to which rebellion against God leads.

Hosea asked the people, "What will you do?" (v. 5). How would the people of Israel respond to God's judgment that

ILLUSTRATOR PHOTO/DAVIDROGERS/THE LOUVRE

Israel put their confidence in Baal, a Canaanite god, rather than the one, true God.

would destroy their nation? More important for us is the question, "How do we respond to God's chastening hand?" An old story tells of two brothers branded with *ST* on their foreheads for being sheep thieves. One brother fled the community in anger only to die without repentance in a far-off land. The other sought God's forgiveness and restoration in the community. He became an example of godly living. Years later when a stranger asked a young man what the *ST* symbolized, he said: "It must mean 'saint.' He is the best man I know."

Judgment for Rejecting God's Prophet (vv. 7-8)

Bursting in on their pagan revelries was not the kind of thing that endeared Hosea to the people. Like other true prophets, Hosea denounced sin without compromise. Like other true prophets, Hosea was hated because of such bold condemnation of sin.

Hosea 9:7-8 has much in common with Amos 7:10-17. Amos was Hosea's contemporary in denouncing Israel's sins. Amos was a plain-spoken man of God who vigorously condemned sin. Amaziah, the priest of Bethel, told the people: "Amos has conspired against you in the midst of the house of Israel; the land is unable to endure all his words" (Amos 7:10). Then Amaziah warned Amos to get out of Israel. Amos declared that God had called him to prophesy. Then Amos proceeded to deliver God's word of sure judgment against Amaziah and Israel.

Hosea 9:7-8 provides one of the few insights into how the Israelites responded to Hosea. His countrymen did not honor him as God's spokesman. They did not turn to God from their sin in response to his message. Rather, they scorned and hated him and plotted his downfall. Instead of a prophet filled with God's Spirit and God's Word, the Israelites preferred court and cult prophets who could be paid to say what they wanted them to say (see Mic. 2:11; 3:5-8).

The people dismissed Hosea as one *demented,* that is, one driven by a fury that could best be described as fanaticism and madness (v. 7).

Why do people reject a true man of God? Hosea told us why: because of their iniquity and hostility (v. 7c). Because of the multitude of their iniquities, the Israelites had a twisted vision of Hosea. They could not see him in his true character as a friend who sought to turn them from death to life.

Hosea described himself as a prophet empowered by God to warn the Israelites to turn from their sin and avoid God's fast-approaching judgment (v. 8). As a prophet, Hosea was God's spokesman. He was like the faithful lookout on the tower of the city wall who sounded the trumpet to warn of the approaching enemy (see Ezek. 33:7).

How do we respond to God's Word to us through His spokesmen? Jesus testified to the fact that people memorialize prophets of the past but reject the prophet through whom God speaks to them (see Matt. 23:29-33). Rather than thank Hosea for his efforts to redeem them, the Israelites treated Hosea as an undesirable wild creature who needed to be removed by trapping (v. 8b).

How will God's true spokesmen respond to the animosity and rejection that they often experience even in God's house? Like Hosea, true gospel ministers will be faithful even under fire. In his story "The Broken Note," Eric P. Kelly described the faithfulness under fire of a young church trumpeter of Krakow, Poland. In the face of invading Tartars, he gave his life to blow a trumpet at the appointed time. As a Tartar arrow pierced his breast, he arose to sound one last glorious note. The church trumpeter today memorializes this young man by breaking off his song in the middle of the note.[2]

Judgment for Depravity (v. 9)

In rejecting God and His prophet through whom God called them to repent, the people plunged deep into depravity. Corruption and perversion are two of the ideas in depravity. In referring to Gibeah, Hosea likened Israel's sin to the perverted sexual sin of certain Benjamites against a Levite and his concubine (see Judg. 19:22,25). Their sin also involved unwillingness on the part of the Benjamites to remove sin from their midst (see Judg. 20:12-13). God's judgment would all but destroy the Israelites of Hosea's day just as God through tribal judgment all but annihilated the Benjamites (see Judg. 20:46-48).

Israel's Persistent Rebellion: Judgment To Sweep Them Away (9:10-17)

A newspaper article told of a 12-foot pet python that wrapped itself around a nine-year-old boy and was trying to swallow him when the paramedics arrived. The boy was home alone when the snake began to coil itself around him. The snake had its mouth around the boy's foot in the process of devouring him. Later, animal control officers confiscated from the house the python as well as a scorpion, two tarantulas, an iguana, and two other large snakes.

The stubborn rebellion that devoured Israel was not new. It became full-blown in Hosea's day. It expressed itself and grew throughout Israel's history. After expressing His initial delight in Israel (v. 10), God described Israel's stubborn rebellion that reared its ugly head first at Baal-peor (vv. 10-14) and then at Gilgal (vv. 15-17).

Israel's Shame at Baal-peor (vv. 10-14)

God used two analogies to express His initial delight in Israel (v. 10). Grapes require careful cultivation. Finding a vine loaded with delicious grapes in the wilderness would be surprising and would bring special delight to a weary, hungry, and thirsty traveler. "The earliest fruit on the fig tree" came from the late sprouts of the previous season and were the best figs (see Jer. 24:2-5).

But from the beginning of Israel's history, the people turned from the God who loved them and gave themselves to shameful idolatry. Baal-peor refers to an event that happened during the wilderness period of Israel's early history. The Israelites' infatuation with the depraved excesses of Baal worship began even before their entrance into Canaan. Read Numbers 25:1-5 to find out what happened.

Shame refers to the shame of fertility worship. People become like the God or gods that they worship. The people of Israel became detestable like the Baal lovers to whom they gave themselves.

Judgment strikes at the heart of sin. The people of Israel gave themselves to calf worship and Baalism to promote their fertility. The Israelites' perceived that *glory* (v. 11) was their numerous children. God, as a direct strike at their fertility gods, would dry up their wombs. Moreover, any children born or already born to them would die "until not a man is left" (v. 12).

The Israelites' true glory was in God's presence with them, but their sin with Baal-peor thwarted His blessings upon them. Now He would depart from them and leave them to the ravages of their sin. Their "woe" (v. 12) would include war that would slaughter their children (v. 13).

Hosea cried out in prayer for his people Israel (v. 14). The only blessing that God could bestow upon such a sinful people is "a miscarrying womb and dry breasts." Then they at least would be spared the tragic death of their newborn children.

Buried in this list of terrible judgments in verses 11-14 is the most terrible judgment of all. The worst woe would be when God Himself departed from them (v. 12). God had loved them and done His best to lead them in the ways of life, but they stubbornly persisted in their choice of the ways of death. God's worst judgment would be to stand aside and let them reap what they had sown.

Israel's Stubborn Rebellion at Gilgal (vv. 15-17)

Israel's actions at Gilgal also mirrored the stubborn rebellion that became full-blown in Hosea's day. At Gilgal, the people of Israel rebelled by rejecting God as their King (see 1 Sam. 8:5-8). Moreover, they refused God's appeal through Samuel to repent (see 1 Sam. 8:9-22). The stubborn rebellion of Saul, Israel's first king, also mirrored the stubborn rebellion of Israel's future kings with the exception of David and those like him (see 1 Sam. 11:15; 13:8-14). A significant fact of Saul's rebellion, seen also in Israel of Hosea's day, was the offering of sacrifices to try to make their disobedience acceptable (see 1 Sam. 15:21-22). Samuel compared their rebellion to witchcraft, idolatry, and other expressions of iniquity to which stubborn rebellion leads (see 1 Sam. 15:23).

As you read verses 15-17, notice the strong words that describe God's attitudes and actions toward the stubborn Israelites. At Gilgal God said, "I came to hate them." Because of their continuing wickedness God "will love them no more" (v. 15). How do we reconcile such statements with the Bible's emphasis on God's love?

The word *hate* does not deny the Bible teaching that God loves sinners; instead it is a way of describing God's abhorrence of sin and what it does to people. By the same token, the words *I will love them no more* do not mean that God ceases to care, but that God's loving entreaties toward sinners do not go on forever. At some point in His dealings with impenitent sinners, God lets them reap what they have sown.

Also keep in mind that God's long-range plan for Israel and later on, Judah, would eventually cause unfaithful Israel to return to the Lord. This was seen in Hosea 2:19-23 and will be seen also in chapters 11—14.

At the same time, the judgment of which Hosea wrote was punitive for the people who had persistently sinned against God's love. Some people believe that God will eventually save all people. This sentimental view of God's love is not the biblical view. God made us free to choose. Such freedom is necessary in order for people to freely choose to love and serve God. Such freedom also means that we can choose to turn our backs on the God of love. At some point, God allows this terrible choice to become final. God withdraws (v. 12) and lets stubborn sinners go their way (v. 17).

Israel's Divided Heart: Destruction of False Institutions (10:1-11)

Modern technology is amazing! I had an electrocardiogram run on my heart as part of a routine exam. The electrocardiogram shows heart irregularities. The test was brief but effective; it took only 11 seconds. It monitored 12 functions of my heart in its 13 beats.

Israel had a bad heart. When God examined Israel's heart He found it to be "faithless" (v. 2). *Faithless* carries two ideas: "divided" and "slippery". The people of Israel did not serve God with all of their hearts. Moreover, their devotion to God was not according to His will. They set up worship practices and rulers who opposed His purposes. The slippery nature of their hearts prevented God from getting hold of their hearts to do His will. Hosea 10:1-11 shows how Israel's cherished institutions would be destroyed because of the peoples' slippery and divided hearts. The two cherished institutions were their religion and their kings. The more God blessed the Israelites, the more altars and pillars they built to express their love for the fertility gods whom they thought made them fruitful (v. 1).

But the time had come for them to "bear their guilt" (v. 2). In particular, God would destroy and remove from them their false worship practices and their false rulers (vv. 2-8). Ultimately, God would bring His people to live in obedience to Him under the Messiah (3:5). For now, God's judgment of eighth-century Israel would be so severe that they would cry out for the mountains and hills to crush and cover them in death rather than to face the continued outpouring of God's wrath (v. 8; Luke 23:30; Rev. 6:16-17).

The people of Israel would eventually recognize that kings other than the Lord could not help them (v. 3). The kings' words were mere empty promises (v. 4). The people, priests, and king would be unable to protect their graven images (vv. 5-6). *Beth-aven* is the scornful name for Bethel. Calf worship made it "a house of emptiness or sin." Already the idol's costly decoration (*glory*) was stripped away to pay tribute to Assyria (v. 5). To the fertility god's shame, the Assyrians would take the calf image to Assyria as a tribute to their king (v. 6).

Samaria (v. 7), the capital city, and the king would fall to the invading Assyrians. The false king and kingdom would be swept away like a branch torn away by lightning and carried away by a fast-moving stream. The same would be the fate of Israel's false worship (v. 8).

The Israelites showed their stubborn hearts at Gibeah (v. 9), and they had not changed over the years. The Israelites' *double guilt* (v. 10) for which God destroyed them may refer only to their religious and political harlotry. My opinion is that the reference is to these sins and to their unwillingness to remove them (see Judg. 19:22,25; 2 Kings 17:6-23).

God's chastisement of the Israelites would come through people gathered against them (v. 10). Israel had been a well-trained heifer with light work and easy grazing (v. 11). Now Israel would bear the heavy yoke of bondage. Judah also was a stubborn heifer and would experience punishment. The larger perspective of chastisement involves all that will happen to the Jewish people until the end of the Gentile age (see Luke 21:24; Rom. 11:25-27).

Israel's Refusal to Repent: Destruction By Devastating War (10:12-15)

Aesop's fable "The Ass and His Driver" pictures the master aided by his sons holding his willful ass by the tail to keep it from plunging headlong over a steep cliff. The ass, resenting his master's interference, pulled the other way until his master was forced to let go his hold. As the ass plunged to its death, the master said: "Well, Jack, if you will be master, you will have to continue on alone."Aesop's point is: a willful beast must go his own way.

Israel was like a willful beast. Its own way was the way of destruction. However, in verse 12 Hosea made one last urgent call to repentance. Fallow ground is once-productive ground presently lying dormant and in disarray.

Hosea suggested three steps to heal the land. "Break up your fallow ground" (v. 12) means to let the plow of repentance sink deeply into the people's hearts to prepare them for the sowing of God's Word. "Sow with a view to righteousness" means putting God's Word into their hearts. Then they would be able to have a personal experience with God that Hosea called "the knowledge of God" (4:1,6; 6:6). "Reap in accordance with kindness" describes the results of the people breaking up their hearts through repentance and of their sowing in their hearts the Word of God.

Kindness is the word for covenant love that means "steadfast and righteous love". The Israelites could still reap the full blessings of covenant love to God and to one another. Their chance to repent, however, was quickly passing. In the expression, "For it is time to seek the Lord," (v. 12) Hosea underscored the urgency of repentance. Their opportunity to repent would soon be gone.

Hosea warned Israel once again of imminent destruction (vv.

13-15). The implication of his warning is that Israel would not repent. The people had and would continue to plow wickedness and to reap a society filled with injustice and deceit. They had and would continue to sow wickedness because they trusted in the military might of their kings instead of trusting in the power of their God. Their trust in military might would destroy them. *Tumult* (v. 14) anticipates the roar and crash of the upcoming battle in which their fortresses would be destroyed and their people brutalized. The reference to Shalman's destroying Beth-arbel is obscure, but it was well-known to Hosea's hearers.

Bethel was the king's sanctuary (see Amos 7:10-13). It epitomized Israel's stubborn rebellion in kingmaking and in licentious worship. In the coming devastation Bethel would experience terrible atrocities. *At dawn* (v. 15) meant that their destruction was a short time away. Then the complete end of their nation would come.

Lessons For Life From Hosea 9:1—10:15

Some of the same basic lessons for life recur throughout the Book of Hosea, but each part of Hosea contains its own way of reinforcing these lessons. Hosea 9:1—10:15 reinforces the basic lesson that persistent sin eventually leads to destruction. Here are some of the ways this basic lesson is expressed:

Sinners sometimes treat with contempt anyone who calls them to repent.—People often profess to honor the prophets of the past, but contemporary prophets are often rejected. This ridicule includes not only preachers but rank-and-file Christians who bear witness to God's Word. Those who would speak God's Word, therefore, must be prepared to continue to speak the truth in love even though some people reject them and their message.

Sin always goes from bad to worse.—It has a way of growing. Thus God warned Cain about his sinful attitude toward Abel: "Sin is crouching at the door; and its desire is for you" (Gen. 4:7). Thus James wrote: "When lust has conceived, it gives birth to sin; and when sin is accomplished, it brings forth death" (Jas. 1:15).

The judgment on sin is separation from God.—By definition, sin is basically going our own way and leaving God out of our lives (Isa. 53:6). This results in a kind of separation from God; however, God seeks sinners (Gen. 3:9; Luke 19:10). God uses every means possible to call sinners to find life by turning to Him; but if sinners persist in rejecting God, at some point God lets them have their way. Hell is eternal separation from God and good.

Now is the urgent time to seek the Lord.—God's mercy and grace are unlimited to those who turn to Him from sin (Ex. 34:6-7). On the other hand, His offer of salvation is limited in time to the unrepentant. "A man who hardens his neck after much reproof will suddenly be broken beyond remedy" (Prov. 29:1).

---

1. Herschel Ford, *Simple Sermons From the Book of Acts*, vol. 2 (Grand Rapids: Zondervan Publishing House, 1950) 127-128.
2. Eric P. Kelly, "The Broken Note," in *Prose and Poetry Journeys*, edited by J. Kenner Agnew (Syracuse: The L. W. Singer Company, Inc.), 279-290.

Personal Learning Activities

1. True ☐ False ☐ Israel, through sinful actions, exemplified the process of national suicide.
2. True ☐ False ☐ One of the seven features of God's judgment was that Israel would go into captivity but not die.
3. Those who escaped to Egypt to avoid Assyrian captivity would ______________________ there.
4. True ☐ False ☐ The prophet in Hosea 9:7-9 was Isaiah.
5. By rejecting God, the prophet, and the call to repentance, Israel plunged deeper into ______________________ .
6. The grapes and the fig tree symbolized ______________ .
7. ______________________________ was the only blessing God could bestow upon a sinful people.
8. The rebellion of Hosea's day was similar to Israel's conduct at ________________.
9. Hosea 10:12 contains a final, urgent call to ___________ .
10. ________________ epitomized Israel's rebellious nature.

Answers: 1. true. 2. false 3. die. 4. false. 5. depravity. 6. God's initial delight in Israel. 7. miscarrying womb and dry breasts. 8. Gilgal. 9. repentance. 10. Bethel.

9

GOD'S COMPASSION FOR HIS PEOPLE

Hosea 11:1—12:14

A compassionate person is one who feels and acts to relieve another's suffering. A parable tells of Compassion and Concern being passengers on an ocean liner. When a man fell overboard, Concern cried: "Man overboard!" Compassion cried, "Man overboard," but jumped into the sea to rescue the imperiled man.

Hosea's message takes a positive turn beginning in chapter 11 and continuing through chapter 14. The Israelites' sin and punishment are still in the forefront. However, the focus in these chapters is upon God's faithful and righteous love by which He would act to save His people. God's compassion toward Israel is foreshadowed and fulfilled in His acting in Christ to redeem all who put their trust in Him.

Summary of 11:1—12:14

As we have studied Hosea, we have noted that Hosea developed four main themes. We have studied three of these: God's faithful love for Israel in spite of their unfaithfulness to Him (1:1—3:5); God's indictment of the sins of unfaithful Israel (4:1—7:16); and the sure judgment that awaited Israel for stubborn refusal to repent (8:1—10:15). Hosea 11:1—14:9 presents the fourth theme: how God's healing love would eventually lead some to repentance and renewal.

Hosea 11:1-11 is a record of God's love in spite of Israel's deceit (vv. 1-4), and of God's love that would use judgment to redeem Israel from deceit (vv. 5-11). Israel's and Judah's problem was their likeness to Jacob, their deceitful forebearer; however,

God would redeem those willing to turn to Him, just as He transformed deceitful Jacob when Jacob wept and sought His favor (11:12—12:6). Israel's bloodguiltiness required terrible judgment, but God would yet bring to pass the redemption symbolized in the Feast of Tabernacles (12:7-14). In the end, God would deliver Israel through the Prophet (Deut. 18:15), just as He delivered and preserved Israel from the Egyptians through a prophet (12:13; see Ex. 3:10; 14:13-31).

God's Nurturing Love (11:1-4)

Two pictures come to mind concerning John Andrew Johnson (my grandson) learning to walk. The first is of my holding out my hands time and time again as Andy took halting steps to walk from his daddy to me. The second is a photograph, proudly displayed by Andy's daddy, showing Andy walking in his daddy's boots. God taught Israel to walk, but Israel did not walk in God's footsteps. Rather, deceitful, treacherous Israel turned from God to follow other gods. Few passages in the Bible describe so graphically as Hosea 11:1-4 the tender, nurturing love of God.

God's Love in Choosing and Caring For Israel (v. 1)

God's love for Israel, and the world He would reach through them, was the basis of His choosing and caring for Israel. The word translated *loved* describes God's redemptive action for Israel as beginning and continuing. In a sense, God loved Israel by choosing and caring for Abraham, Isaac, and Jacob, Israel's ancestors. God continued His love for the people in calling them out of Egypt into covenant with Himself. In the covenant He would be their God and they would be His people (Ex. 19:4-6). They were already His "firstborn" when He called them out of Egypt (Ex. 4:22). God's desire was that they should become like Him.

God's Love in Spite of Israel's Deceit (vv. 2-4)

God had been to Israel throughout their existence like a loving father, a faithful husband, and a compassionate farmer. Israel had been to God as a prodigal son (v. 2), an unfaithful wife

(1:2; 2:2; 3:1), and a stubborn heifer (4:16). "The more they called them" (v. 2) probably refers to the prophets through whom God persistently sought to lead the people to trust and obey Him. "The more they went from them" pictures the people turning increasingly from the prophets with each appeal the prophets made for the people to turn back to God.

"I . . . taught Ephraim to walk" (v. 3) depicts God as a Father teaching His child to walk, that is, to trust and to obey Him. Moses probably had in mind the figure "I took them in My arms" in his saying: "And in the wilderness where you saw how the Lord your God carried you just as a man carries his son" (Deut. 1:31). Moses probably referred to the wonders God performed for the people of Israel in leading them from the Red Sea to Mount Sinai. The Israelites in their hardness of heart were blind to God as the real source of their blessings.

God used two analogies to show His continued love for Israel (v. 4). "With cords of a man, with bonds of love" may continue the picture of God as a Father teaching His child to walk, but I believe the analogy pictures God as a faithful Husband. *I led them* refers to God's repeated acts by which He sought to weave and bind Israel's heart to His own.

The analogy of lifting "the yoke from their jaws" seems to picture God as a compassionate farmer. The focus is upon two of His compassionate actions: tenderly yoking them in service and graciously feeding them. God had yoked Ephraim in His service. However, He carefully placed the yoke on their necks and jaws so that they did not feel the pressure. Then He took off the yoke and placed food before them so that they could eat and rest.

God's Promise of Restoration (11:5-11)

Israel's sins and God's love are set against each other throughout Hosea. This is especially true in the final chapters. Hosea 11:1-4 describes how Israel sinned against God's love. Hosea 11:5-11 shows how God's love persisted in spite of Israel's stubborn sins. Their stubborn rebellion doomed them as a nation (vv. 5-7), but God refused to give up on Israel (vv. 8-9). His redemptive love would ultimately triumph (vv. 10-11).

Hosea pictured Assyria as a death army, ready to destroy Israel because of the nations's sins. "And the sword will whirl against their cities . . . and consume them because of their counsels." (11:6)

Results of Rejecting God's Love (vv. 5-7)

The Israelites brought a threefold tragedy on themselves in persistently despising God's love. First was the Assyrian Captivity (v. 5). Previously, Hosea used *Egypt* to symbolize the land of bondage (8:13; 9:3). The Israelites, who had and would flee to Egypt to escape the Assyrian Captivity, would die in Egypt (9:6). The land of bondage would not be Egypt itself but Assyria. Hosea used a play on words to show that the people of Israel would *return* to captivity, because they willfully and persistently refused to *return* to God.

The second tragic result was continued desolation of the Israelites and their land (v. 6). The Assyrian scourge would continue until it made a full end of the Northern Kingdom. Desolation would come because the people followed *their counsels* instead of the counsel God gave them through the prophets.

The third and most tragic result was that their rejecting God's love led them to a state of fixed rebellion against God (v. 7). "Are bent on turning from Me" pictures Israel's fixed apostasy. "Like a stubborn heifer" (4:16), the people of Israel slid backward on their haunches as God tenderly sought to yoke them in His service.

"The One on high" refers to God. The people brought a degree of hardness to their hearts every time they refused to respond to God's appeal to them through His prophets. Finally, they became totally set in rebellion against God. "None at all" does not include persons like Hosea who were godly. The nation as a whole was now united in hardened rebellion against God.

God's Persistent Love for Israel (vv. 8-9)

Martin Luther said, "If I were God, I would kick the world to pieces." Thank God that God is God, not man.

The questions in verse 8 should be read with great pathos so as to express the struggle going on in God's heart. The issue was not whether He would punish Israel, but whether He would cut them off forever from being His people and from living in His land.

"How can I give you up, O Ephraim?" and the following three questions imply a negative answer. God would in no way annihilate them. Admah and Zeboiim, like Sodom and Gomorrah, were cities in the vale of Siddim that God destroyed, never to rise again (Gen. 14:2,8; Deut. 29:23). The thought of giving up His people to annihilation produced an outburst of compassion in God's heart.

Verse 9 expresses God's pledge not to change His mind about showing mercy and grace to the people of Israel. He was now set in His determination to find a way to redeem them. The Israelites' sin placed the severest stress on God's nature. Their sin demanded punishment. Moreover, God would not forgive them unless they would follow Him and trust and obey Him. God in His divine nature would find a way to redeem Israel.

God would temper His *fierce anger* (v. 9) with His mercy and grace. With measured control God would send adversaries like the Assyrians to judge them. Through such judgment God would open up their hearts to His redemptive love.

The Triumph of God's Love (vv. 10-11)

Verses 10-11 express God's promise that Israel one day would walk in His footsteps. *Will walk* denotes the returning process as beginning and continuing until complete.

From the west is literally "from the sea," that is, from the direction of the Mediterranean Sea. Thus, the Israelites' ultimate dispersion for their sin would be larger than the Assyrian captivity and even the Babylonian captivity (see Deut. 30:3; Isa. 43:5-7; Luke 21:24). Returnees from the Assyrian and Babylonian captivities would come from the East and then north around the Fertile Crescent. Egyptian returnees would come from the South.

Israel of Hosea's day was like "a silly dove, without sense" (7:11). They vacillated between Assyria and Egypt in their search for help. In the time of their redemption, Israel would return from the place of their dispersion like migrating birds returning to their home.

God promised to "settle them in their houses." A literal translation of this promise is: "And I will cause them to return to their houses." *Their houses* refers to the dwelling places in God's land from which God would drive them.

An important fact concerning God is that He loves Israel, and He loves righteousness (Deut. 7:7-8; Psalm 11:7). How can God love the sinful Israelites and commit Himself to redeem them (3:1-5)? The answer is in God's nature. As the Holy One in the midst of Israel, God would find a way to transform the Israelites from their fixed state of rebellion into an obedient people who would walk after Him (v. 10).

God's Call to Be Changed (11:12—12:6)

Israel's Deceit and Treachery (11:12—12:1)

Two examples come quickly to mind when I think of deceitful and treacherous people. One is Judas Iscariot, who betrayed the Savior with a kiss (Luke 6:16; 22:48). The other is Benedict Arnold, who betrayed our country at the time of our war for independence.

In 11:12—12:1 we are brought back to where Israel and Judah were in Hosea's day. They both were deceitful and treacherous people. Judah most likely recently experienced the revival that took place under King Hezekiah (2 Kings 18:4-6), but Ephraim was probably in its last days. Indeed, the Northern Kingdom was destroyed in the sixth year of Hezekiah's reign (2 Kings 18:9-10). In a sense, Judah was yet faithful to God (11:12, KJV). However, the seeds of deceit, treachery, and death were in Judah as well as Israel (12:2).

God, who dwelt in His people's midst (11:9), looked for the faithfulness and kindness that He gives to those who know Him personally (4:1). Instead, God found Himself surrounded by deceitful and treacherous people. Their deceit and treachery was in contrast to God—the Holy One—who is faithful.

By their covenants with Assyria and Egypt, Israel committed political harlotry against God with whom they were bound in covenant. Israel betrayed God by looking to Assyria and Egypt for protection, guidance, and life-style. Their political harlotry paralleled their spiritual harlotry in turning from God to follow fertility gods.

Their deceitful and treacherous policies were futile and destructive. *Feeding on wind* is impossible and thus futile. *Pursuing the east wind* is destructive. *Lies and violence* (12:1) are emphatic in the Hebrew text to magnify the results of their deceit and treachery.

An Example of Rebellion and Return (12:2-6)

Years ago, Sam Cannata, veteran medical missionary to Southern Rhodesia, testified: "I stand before you today with only one eye, but it's God's eye." Cannata told how an African lad coughed into his eye as he bent over the lad to treat him. Cannata sought treatment for the infection, but the disease took away his sight in that eye. Surprisingly, Cannata thanked God for the bad experience, because he became through it totally dedicated to God.[1]

God's controversy with His people included the Southern Kingdom (Judah) (11:12; 12:2) as well as the Northern Kingdom (Ephraim). *Jacob* (v. 2) is the personal name for the patriarch from whom Israel's twelve tribes descended.

Jacob means "trickster or supplanter." The name is built on the Hebrew word for heel. Jacob was so named because he came out of the womb holding to Esau's heel (Gen. 25:26). The name suggests that Jacob used deceit and treachery to take what he wanted. His redeeming quality was his desire for God and the spiritual birthright and blessing that comes from being chosen by God.

Jacob sought God and His blessings through his own self-will. In the womb he pulled Esau by the heel in an effort to replace Esau as firstborn (Gen. 25:22-26). As a boy, Jacob seized upon Esau's hunger and spiritual indifference to purchase Esau's birthright with a bowl of pottage (Gen. 25:29-34). As a young man, he tricked his aged father Isaac into pronouncing upon him the firstborn blessing (Gen. 27:35-36). As a mature man,

Jacob sought in an act of absolute self-will to overpower God Himself (Gen. 32:24-32).

The angel (v. 4) with whom Jacob wrestled at the ford of the Jabbok was the Person through whom God personally manifested Himself. Accordingly, Jacob called the place *Peniel*, which means "the face of God" (Gen. 32:30). Many interpreters identify this Person as the preincarnate Christ. To Jacob's credit, he would not let God go until He blessed him (Gen. 32:26). Jacob prevailed with God and men only when he yielded himself to God. God's chastisement was the catalyst producing Jacob's yielding. God crippled Jacob by touching the socket of Jacob's thigh (Gen. 32:25).

God broke Jacob's self-will at Peniel. The transformation Jacob could never achieve through his own self-strivings came when he yielded himself to God. God symbolized the transformation by changing Jacob's name to *Israel*, meaning "prince of God" (Gen. 32:28, KJV).

Notice that Hosea wrote, "He spoke with us" (v. 4). God revealed Himself to Jacob at Bethel and spoke with all Israel who at the time were in Jacob's loins. There God affirmed Jacob's transformation into Israel (Gen. 35:1-12). God's particular promise is that He would not leave Jacob and his descendants until He accomplished all that He promised concerning them (Gen. 28:15). Included was the promise to be with him and his descendants, to keep him and his descendants, and to bring him and them back into the land. God transformed Jacob into Israel by bringing him back into the land from Paddan-aram. God would transform Jacob's posterity into true Israelites by bringing them back into the land from worldwide dispersion (Deut. 30:1-10).

In verse 5 God gave His name as the memorial that assures the fulfillment of His promises to redeem the Jacob people. "The God of hosts" points to God's absolute power. "LORD" is *Yahweh*, God's personal name. His name identifies Him as the One Who Causes To Be. As such, God is the one who would bring about Israel's promised redemption. God's faithfulness to Himself and to His redemptive promises is also the guarantee of our salvation.

Hosea spelled out the way for people to be changed as Jacob

was changed (v. 6). This important verse stresses three truths about being changed: (1) Turning to God from sin is the beginning point. *Return to God* refers to this kind of true repentance. (2) God expects those who turn to Him to live with *kindness* and *justice*. A covenant with God involves practicing the qualities of God Himself. (3) The ability to practice kindness and justice comes from personal experience with God. Turning to God leads to fellowship with God and strength from Him to live as God expects. *Wait for your God* means "to weave your life completely around God."

God's Redemption of Israel (12:7-14)

Corrupt Goals of a Corrupt Nation (vv. 7-8)

God would bring about a new day for the people of Israel, but people of Hosea's day were corrupt to the core. They expressed their corruption through their goals. They no longer cared for their covenant goals of being "a kingdom of priests and a holy nation" (Ex. 19:6). Their desire was to be wealthy merchants by whatever means were necessary.

Hosea accused the wealthy merchants of dishonesty and oppression in order to get rich. Hosea's words about *false balances* (v. 7) repeat a similar warning by Amos about merchants who cheated by using "dishonest scales to make the bushel smaller and the shekel bigger" (Amos 8:5). In other words, they sold less than they claimed at more than it was worth. *Oppress* means "to take by force." Amos wrote that the poor were the victims of these greedy, dishonest merchants (Amos 2:6-7; 8:6).

Thus they were guilty of the opposite of the kindness and justice that God shows to people and that He expects of His people. Dishonest exploitation is the opposite of kindness and justice.

The crooked merchants added denial to their sin. Although they readily admitted acquiring great wealth, they denied wrongdoing in the practices used to acquire their wealth (v. 8).

Judgment and Redemption Pictured and Affirmed (vv. 9-10)

The people were corrupt to the core. Yet God was still Israel's God, and He would redeem them. God would make Israel "live in tents again, as in the days of the appointed festival." Reference probably is to the Feast of Tabernacles (Booths). The booths in which the people dwelt during the festival symbolized the wilderness wandering from which God redeemed His people. The festival itself pictured pure, simple, and beautiful life with God.

God's making the Israelites "live in tents again" implies the coming dispersion followed by restoration. The time would come when God would regather His people, purify them from their sin, make them one with Him, and then dwell with them forever. These events are symbolized respectively in the Feast of Trumpets, the Day of Atonement, and the Feast of Tabernacles.

God spoke through His prophets such as Hosea and Amos to affirm His ultimate redemption of Israel (v. 10). Amos' visions provide examples of the numerous visions God gave to His prophets affirming Israel's redemption. In his visions, Amos saw that God's judgment of Israel was certain and imminent (Amos 7:7-9; 8:1-3). God would put to death the sinners of His people, but He would not totally destroy His people. He would sift them in judgment as grain is shaken in a sieve, but not a kernel would fall to the ground (see Amos 9:8-10).

Hosea provides an example of prophetic similitudes (*parables*). God directed Hosea to take a wife who became unfaithful to Hosea as Israel was unfaithful to God (1:2). Then God commanded Hosea to love her according to the love with which God loves Israel. In Hosea's purchase and discipline of Gomer according to God's command, Hosea pictured the loving action by which God would redeem faithless Israel (3:1-5).

Bearing Guilt; Redemption Through the Prophet (vv. 11-14)

Hosea once again used Jacob to illustrate Israel's redemption (vv. 12-13). In his self-will, Jacob had to flee to Paddan-aram from the promised land to escape Esau's wrath. There he experienced in Laban's dealings with him the same deceit and treachery he had given to others (Gen. 29—31). Jacob's self-will, which he reproduced in his descendants, led to Israel's bondage in Egypt. In God's time God delivered and preserved

Israel by Moses, the prophet and leader of His people.

In like manner, the Israelites of Hosea's day would suffer for their sin. In God's own time, He would send forth the Prophet in the likeness of Moses who would deliver His people from sin and bring them into true covenant with God. The Prophet is the Lord Jesus Christ (see Deut. 18:15; Acts 3:20-22).

Lessons for Life from Hosea 11:1—12:14

God lovingly seeks to care for and lead people in the ways of life.—A familiar child's prayer begins, "God is great and God is good." This blessing focuses on the twofold emphasis of the biblical revelation of God. He is the powerful, infinite, eternal God—Creator of all things. He is the gracious, good, and merciful Heavenly Father.

Sin breaks the heart of God.—As noted earlier, sin is not brave rebellion against a tyrannical, uncaring deity. It is rejection of the lovingkindness of the Heavenly Father. Most people at some time experience the pain of rejected love. The deep hurt we feel should help us have better insight into the pain that sin causes God. The cross is the ultimate expression of that pain.

A changed life is possible by God's grace and power.—Sinners cannot change their lives without experiencing God's mercy and presence. But through His grace and help, we can break with the past and enter a new life. Bible examples—like Jacob and Paul—show how God transforms.

God calls His people to practice kindness and justice.—God Himself is kind and just. He calls His people to be kind and just. As Micah 6:8 puts it: "And what does the LORD require of you but to do justice, to love kindness, and to walk humbly with your God?

---

1. Cal Guy, ". . . but it's God's eye," *Baptist Standard*, 11 September 1963.

Personal Learning Activities

1. During Israel's existence, God had been like (3 things): ________, ________, ________.
2. Israel, in contrast, had been like (3 things): ________, ________, ________.
3. What were the three tragedies Israel brought on herself? ________, ________, ________
4. True ☐ False ☐ God would find a way to transform Israel from a rebellious state into obedience.
5. Compassion means: loving action ☐ sorrow ☐ concern ☐.
6. Rather than faithfulness and kindness, God found His people to be ________ and ________.
7. How did Israel commit *political* harlotry against God? ________
8. With whom did God have a dispute due to his rebellion? ________
9. The Israelites expressed corruption through their ________.
10. The Festival of Tabernacles (Booths) pictured ________.

Answers: 1. loving father, faithful husband, compassionate farmer. 2. prodigal son, unfaithful wife, stubborn heifer. 3. Assyrian captivity, continued desolation of the people and land, rejecting God's love resulting in fixed rebellion against God. 4. true. 5. sorrow. 6. deceitful, treacherous. 7. looked to Assyria and Egypt for guidance, protection, and life-style. 8. Jacob. 9. goals. 10. pure, simple, beautiful life with God.

10

God's Healing Love

Hosea 13:1—14:9

In an earlier chapter I described cutting down an oak tree in my backyard. I was forced to cut it down because the wind could have blown the rotten tree onto my house. A stump was left after the rotten tree was cut down. What I did not mention earlier is that shoots of new life are coming up out of that hollow stump. These shoots give hope of a strong oak tree in years to come.

Much of the Book of Hosea focuses on the sure judgment of God on the stubbornly sinful nation of Israel. However, mixed with the messages of judgment are messages of hope. God's judgments are sometimes punitive; that is, those who persistently reject God's love are eventually condemned to reap what they have sown. But as long as sinners have the possibility of repentance, God's judgments have a redemptive purpose. God uses both blessings (Rom. 2:4) and chastisements (Heb. 12:11-12) to show His love and to call people to repentance.

The Book of Hosea clearly predicted the fall of Israel as a nation, but Hosea presented a message of hope based on God's healing love. For one thing, although the nation was doomed, God offered Himself to individual Israelites who could still repent. Even more important, the doom of Israel as a nation did not mean the end of God's redemptive purposes. To the contrary, the message of God's healing love in Hosea is fulfilled in God's saving purpose for His people through His Son Jesus Christ.

Summary of 13:1—14:9

The emphasis in Hosea 13 is primarily—but not exclusively—on the doom of Israel as a nation. Ephraim went from glory to shame (13:1-3). Although God wanted to save Israel, sin would force Him to be Israel's destroyer (13:4-8). Israel had turned from God as King to kings who brought only ruin (13:9-11). Although judgment was about to be poured out on Israel, God reaffirmed His purpose to redeem His people (13:12-16). The theme of God's healing love is clear and strong in Hosea 14. God called for repentance based on His grace and mercy (14:1-3). God promised to pour out this love on His repentant people (14:4-8). The book ends with an exhortation to exercise wisdom by walking in the Lord's ways (14:9).

From Glory to Shame (13:1-3)

Ephraim was the largest and most important of the northern tribes. Its key city Samaria was the Northern Kingdom's capital. As such, Hosea sometimes used *Ephraim* to stand for the Northern Kingdom (5:13). In Hosea 13:1, however, Hosea seems to have concentrated on the tribe of Ephraim. Ephraim's movement from glory to shame illustrates what happened as a whole to the nation.

God looked back to the time when Ephraim trembled before Him in humble submission to His will (v. 1). As the result Ephraim exalted himself among Israel's twelve tribes, so that the other tribes *trembled* in respect when Ephraim spoke. Out of this God-honoring tribe came Joshua (Num. 13:8,16). Then God chose Joshua to succeed Moses and to lead Israel on to victory (Num. 27:15-23).

When Ephraim turned from God (v. 1), out of Ephraim's bosom came Jeroboam the son of Nebat. Jeroboam led Israel to embrace the golden calf cult that brought death to the Northern Kingdom (1 Kings 11:26; 12:25-33; 2 Kings 17:20-23).

The Northern Kingdom's death process was slow but final. It began when the people deserted the Lord to follow the fertility gods. It continued and grew worse as each succeeding generation refused to repent at the call of God through the prophets (2 Kings 17:13-14). Death's climax would soon come by Assyria's burial of Israel forever as a nation. The fall occurred in 722 B.C. when the Assyrians took Samaria and carried surviving Israelites into the Assyrian Captivity (2 Kings 17:5-7).

God focused on Ephraim's present apostasy in saying "and now"(v. 2). Like other generations of Israelites, they refused God's call to repentance and sinned "more and more." Ephraim was like the walking dead, seeking life in the fertility gods that bring death.

Kissing the calf and Baal images was one aspect of fertility worship. However, "the men who sacrifice" may be translated "the sacrificers of men." Certainly, some sacrificed children to "the idols of Canaan" (Ps. 106:38; 2 Kings 21:6). The sacrificial method is not known. Some think that parents threw their children into a raging fire in the god's bosom. Others picture the parents as binding their children in the image's arms, which was then fired from below. Some hold that worshipers pounded drums to drown out the children's cries.

Therefore (v. 3) points to the cumulative result of Israel's sin. A man's glory is whatever gives him weight and honor among his fellowmen. The true worship of God led Ephraim to great honor among its neighbors, but the once-glorious nation would now soon disappear as a nation.

From God as Savior to God as Destroyer (13:4-8)

This passage includes both a description of God as savior (vv. 4-5) and God as a ravenous beast stalking and tearing the flock (vv. 7-8). The Savior became the destroyer because the Israelites rejected their God (v. 6).

With the words *Yet I*, God contrasted His uninterrupted care of Israel with their apostasy toward Him (v. 4). *Since the land of Egypt* marks the time when the Lord adopted Israel as a nation to be His people and He became their God. He demonstrated His love for them and His faithfulness to His promise to their father Abraham in delivering them from Egypt (Gen. 15:13-17).

God would not tolerate the people of Israel having another god. There is really no other god for the people of Israel or for anyone else to follow. The Lord God of Israel is the only God. Israel's experience illustrates this truth. In Israel's history, no other god had demonstrated actual power on the Israelites' behalf. Only God demonstrated the ability to save. Even when the people of Israel attributed their deliverance and well-being to other gods, God alone was their benefactor (2:8; 11:3).

God also personally loved and cared for them in their wilderness journey (v. 5) and brought them into the promised land. The wilderness of Sinai was a land of great hardship. *Their pasture* (v. 6) denotes the land of Canaan.

Before the Israelites entered Canaan, God through Moses warned them of the peril of prosperity. Turn to Deuteronomy 8:11-14 and read that grave warning. Notice that Hosea 13:6 shows how the Israelites ignored the warning.

After the Good Shepherd brought them into the good land that flowed with milk and honey, they forgot Him. *And being satisfied* carries the idea of being satiated from gorging themselves on God's good provision. *Their heart became proud* illustrates the evil results of proud self-sufficiency that often flows from prosperity (Prov. 1:31-32). Instead of loving and trusting God their benefactor, they attributed His blessings to the fertility gods and turned from Him to follow them.

Verses 7-8 indicate that God changed His role toward the people of Israel from loving Shepherd of the flock to ravaging beast devouring the flock as the result of their forsaking Him. In their hardness of heart, the Israelites would no longer respond favorably to God's goodness. His only course to draw out trust and obedience from them was the severe punishment of national extinction and exile.

God used three analogies to describe Himself as ravaging beast devouring the flock. The first likened Him to a lion. The lion's ferocity is well known. The second referred to God as a leopard lying "in wait by the wayside." God depicted Himself as lying concealed in the way along which the flock would go, ready to pounce upon them. The third analogy depicted God as "a bear robbed of her cubs." A mother bear is an especially dangerous animal.

God's judgment would leave Israel like a devoured sheep carcass. God's judgment would tear away Israel's protection to devour the heart. Then wild beasts would pick the carcass clean. The point is this: God's judgment would lead to the Northern Kingdom's death. However, the divine Shepherd would recover from the devouring beast as it were "a couple of legs or a piece of ear" (Amos 3:12). From this remnant God could and would fulfill His redemptive purpose (Amos 9:8-15; see Acts 15:15-18, which quotes Amos 9:11-12).

From God as King to Destructive Leaders (13:9-11)

An Aesop's fable tells of frogs who chose first a log and then a stork to be their king. King Log made a big splash when it fell into the water. Its impotence led to the frogs regarding it with contempt. King Stork was worse. It ate up the frogs as fast as it could. When the frogs called out for help, the only answer that

ILLUSTRATOR PHOTO/DAVID ROGERS

Like a lion, the "king of beasts," God would devour Israel in judgment. "So I will be like a lion to them." (13:7)

came was that they would suffer the punishment due to their folly.

Verses 9-11 present translation difficulties as the various versions indicate. The sense, however, is clear. God and God alone was and is Israel's help (v. 9). The people of Israel destroyed themselves by turning from God as King to follow after impotent, destructive leaders. All of Israel's kings followed Jeroboam I the son of Nebat in promoting calf worship in the name of the Lord God of Israel. As such, they set themselves and their nation against their God.

God Himself stands determined to be king over Israel (v. 10, KJV). The people of Israel made God angry by requesting a king to rule over them in the place of God (v. 11). Their final corruption was so complete that God in His wrath would now destroy them and their king. The question "where now is your king" (v. 10) implies that the Assyrians by this time had taken as a prisoner Hoshea, Israel's last king (2 Kings 17:4).

God's Determination to Save Through Judgment (13:12-16)

Ephraim's sin was full and ready for God's judgment (v. 12; see Gen. 15:16; Lev. 18:24-25). *Bound up* and *stored up* suggest that Israel's guilt and punishment were on file before God like an irrevocable death penalty.

God likened the judgment He was about to send upon Israel to a travailing woman's birth pangs (v. 13). As such, the judgment would be intended to give new birth to Israel.

Israel of Hosea's day resisted stubbornly God's efforts to redeem them. Israel was like an unwise son who would die because of refusal to be born. *He is not a wise son* implies that Israel was responsible for their tragic dilemma.

How would God respond to the Israelites' dilemma? Their end would be death forever unless He acted to redeem them. What would He do? He would not cut them off forever from being His people. Rather, He would take the steps to "ransom them from the power of Sheol" and to "redeem them from death."

Differences of opinion exist about how to translate the last part of 13:14. "Compassion will be hidden from My sight" (NASB) means that the Lord would not redeem Israel of Hosea's day from the destruction and death caused by Israel's sins. "Repentance shall be hid from mine eyes" (KJV) looks past Israel of Hosea's day whose national life God would bring to an end (vv. 15-16). It affirms God's determination as the Holy God in the midst of Israel to find a way to redeem Israel (11:9).

My translation of 13:14 with focus on God's determination to redeem Israel is:

From the hand of Sheol, I am determined to ransom them.
From death, I am determined to redeem them.
O death, I am determined to be thy plagues.
O Sheol, I am determined to be thy destruction.
Repentance will be hidden from my eyes.

Sheol is the Hebrew word for the realm of the departed spirits. It is the place into which people pass at death. The Greek word for *Sheol* is *Hades.* The larger biblical concept, which God surely knew when He used the word *Sheol* in Hosea's day, includes heaven and hell (Luke 16:19-31). *Death* ultimately involves eternal punishment in hell ("the second death") for those who refuse God's redemption (Rev. 20:13-15). Taken together in the larger biblical context, *Sheol* and *death* picture sin's power to demand the penalty of eternal death. In the case of the people of Hosea's day, *Sheol* and *death* would be the power of their sin to destroy them forever as God's people.

God declared His determination to redeem Israel. In the larger biblical context, we know that God is able to ransom and to redeem from death because He, acting in Christ, paid the price for our sin and was raised from the dead (Titus 2:14; 1 Pet. 2:24). Paul put together God's promises here and in Isaiah 25:8 to mock *death* and *Sheol* in view of Christ's redemptive work. He saw complete victory over sin, death, and the grave for all who put their trust in Christ. (See 1 Cor. 15:54-57).

The usual word for *repentance* means "to return" (14:1). The word used for *repentance* in verse 14 means "to grieve over other's misery." It involves taking action that brings comfort to oneself by bringing comfort to those in misery. God would bring comfort to His own grieving heart and comfort to Israel by standing firm in His decision ultimately to redeem Israel (11:9).

Hosea came back in verses 15-16 to underscore the terrible judgment God was about to bring upon the people of Hosea's day. *An east wind* (the sirocco) is both violent and scorching. The figure stands for Assyria, but it is "the wind of the Lord" (v. 15), because God would make Assyria His instrument for punishing Israel. The violent, scorching wind would dry up Israel's source of life and fruitfulness. It also would take away all that brought delight to Israel.

Samaria, the capital of the Northern Kingdom, was the fountainhead of the nation's rebellion against God. As such, Samaria would bear the brunt of God's devastating judgment of war with all its brutalities (v. 16; 2 Kings 17:5-6).

Call to True Repentance (14:1-3)

When does one truly repent? Several years ago my wife and I were traveling through Atlanta, Georgia. Detours took us into downtown Atlanta where I got lost. Getting lost was my fault. My wife told me to turn right; I chose to go straight ahead. There was some confusion, but I settled the issue by saying: "I'm the captain of this ship. We'll go straight ahead."

Before long the road narrowed, and I began to doubt that I had chosen the right road. Then the road took on a residential look, and I knew I had made a mistake. My face began to burn as I thought about admitting my error. All the time my wife was telling me that I should turn around and go back. Finally, I did turn around, went back to the intersection, and got on the right road.

The question is: when did I repent? Was it when I began to doubt that I had taken the right road? Was it when I knew I had made a mistake? Was it when I began to burn over my error? No! I repented when I turned around, went back to the intersection, and got on the right road.

Hosea looked forward to the time when Israel would repent. In his call, Hosea both encouraged Israel to return to the Lord and told them how to return (vv. 2-3).

Return (v. 1) is the word for true repentance, which would be going back to God, acknowledgment of sin, sorrow for sin, and restoration from sin. Hosea used the words *O Israel* to address all of the people as a single person in his exhortation to turn back to God. The nation could come back to God only as individual Israelites returned to God. Accordingly, Hosea shifted to the plural in verse 2 to call all Israelites as individuals back to God. Particularly, he instructed each of them how to return to the Lord. Rather than go back with rams and lambs for sacrifice, he told them to take with them "words" (v. 2) expressive of a truly repentant heart.

Hosea provided a model prayer of repentance in verses 2-3. *Take away all iniquity* is literally "to lift up and bear away." It is the word used to describe complete removal of sin as symbolized in the scapegoat on the Day of Atonement (Lev. 16:20-22). *And receive us graciously* is a request for God to give to them the restoration they needed but did not deserve. *That we may present the fruit of our lips* is the pledge of the repentant Israelites to offer verbally the praise and thanksgiving in their hearts.

Hosea continued the model prayer in verse 3. Throughout their history, the people of Israel rejected God by (1) depending on alliances with other nations for their security, (2) desiring for security in military might as symbolized by *horses*, and (3) trusting in the fertility gods as the source of their blessings. By rejecting all these, there is the implication that they would now totally trust and obey God forever.

Notice the final words in verse 3: "For in Thee the orphan finds mercy." With these words the Israelites would explain the reason that they would no longer manufacture their own gods, trust in military might, and/or depend on foreign powers for their security. They as individuals and as a nation would have found in God the salvation they desperately needed.

After True Repentance (14:4-8)

God describes in verses 4-8 the immediate and loving response He would make to the repentant people of Israel. This is the same response that God makes to anyone who sincerely turns to Him. First, He would "heal their apostasy" (v. 4). God would change their hearts and rid them forever of the immorality that brought their ruin.

Second, God would "love them freely." God's love would be the means of His healing them. Moreover, after healing them He could love them willingly and generously without any hindrance. God's wrath would be *turned away* because in their returning to God He would heal them from their apostasy.

Third, God would bless them profusely (vv. 5-8). God used seven flourishing plant-life descriptions to picture the growth and blessings that He would bring to pass for repentant Israel. The first four descriptions picture what redeemed Israel would be. The next two picture redeemed Israel's impact on others. The final description pictures what God would be to redeemed Israel.

The lily symbolizes the beauty and purity that would characterize Israel. Like the cedars of Lebanon, Israelites would be rooted in God and in the land and would spread upward and outward in new growth. They also would exude a sweet odor to God and to fellowmen. Like the olive tree, they would be bright and fruitful.

Those who live in his shadow seems to refer to those who live under redeemed Israel's influence. These would revive as grain and blossom as grape-bearing vines.

God would be to redeemed Israel like "a luxuriant cypress." Redeemed Israel would turn forever from fertility gods or any other form of idolatry. God Himself in His perpetual care of them would respond to all their needs.

Ephraim (Israel) had been a luxuriant vine producing fruit for himself (10:1). Israel would bring forth God's fruit as the result of abiding in Him. Israel, thus, would fulfill in the end Christ's ideal for all of His people (John 15:1-11).

A Word to the Wise (14:9)

You may remember the often repeated story of the steamboat worker who pointed with love and joy to the captain of another boat as their boats passed on the Mississippi River. The worker explained: "Several years ago I fell overboard in these waters. I was about to drown when that captain jumped in and rescued me. Ever since then, I have loved to point him out."

God, through His redeeming love, saved Hosea, Hosea's wayward wife, and their home. Hosea envisioned the day when God would redeem even the nation of Israel, God's wayward people.

Through the prophecy that bears his name, Hosea pointed in love and joy to the Savior. He closed his book with an encouragement for all who read to understand and experience in their own lives the triumph of God's redeeming love.

God's ways are straight and lead to redemption in Christ Jesus. The wise and discerning show their wisdom and discernment by walking in the way of God's redeeming love. The foolish alternative is to stumble in rebellion. That leads to eternal destruction. Are you wise or foolish?

Lessons For Life From Hosea 13:1—14:9

God promises healing to the repentant.—God's quick and loving response to repentant Israel illustrates how He will heal us when we turn to Him from our sin. He is the Great Physician who can heal the sin-sick soul.

God's love is both tender and tough.—Most of us have heard about "tough love" as a strategy for helping people, especially rebellious children. In a sense, God uses tough love in trying to awaken rebellious sinners to their moral and spiritual need. God's basic way of showing love is through tender mercies and blessings; but when necessary, God uses chastisements to bring conviction of need.

Repentance means changing direction in life.—Conviction and godly sorrow are involved; but unless sinners turn to God and from sin, repentance does not take place. Sinners must recognize they are going the wrong direction in life and turn around and go the other direction. The deadliness of sin makes repentance necessary. The grace and power of God make it possible.

God's redemptive purpose will triumph.—God, not sin, will win the final victory. This does not mean that God will finally save all people—regardless of their sins and of their own choices. Sin and salvation, heaven and hell are realities. God made us free in order that we might choose Him, but He knew that some would use this freedom to reject Him.

The triumph of God's love means that God's love will triumph in the lives of His people and in the destiny of the universe. On the surface, sin and unbelief often seem to be winning; but people of faith believe the revelations of God's Word. We see the revelation of God's triumph in various ways in the Old Testament, but we see it most clearly in the cross and resurrection. We see God's love shining through the horrors of the crucifixion (Rom. 5:6-8). And we see this victory sealed through the resurrection of Jesus Christ from the dead (1 Cor. 15:55-57). The final fulfillment of God's redemptive purpose is sure (Phil. 2:6-11).

Personal Learning Activities

1. "Baal" (v. 1) stands for ______________________.
2. God (v. 4) contrasted His uninterrupted care of Israel with ______________________
3. Savior means ______________________.
4. God changed His role from Shepherd to ______________ in Hosea 13:4-8.
5. God compared the ______________ He would send upon Israel to a ______________. Thus, the ______________ would be intended to give ______________ to Israel.
6. ***Sheol*** is a word for (choose *all* correct answers): (a) heaven, (b) realm of the departed spirits, (c) place into which people pass at death, (d) purgatory.
7. What is God's response to all who repent? (3 answers) ______________, ______________, ______________
8. Write your own paraphrase of Hosea 14:9. ______________________
9. List three things you learned from your study of Hosea. ______________________
10. Choose one of those things and write a short essay on how you can apply it to your life.

Answers: 1. all fertility gods embraced by Israel. 2. their apostasy toward God. 3. one who rescues from evil and/or death to safety and well-being. 4. raging beast. 5. judgment, women's birth pangs, judgment, new birth. 6. b, c. 7. heal their apostasy, love them freely, bless them. 8. personal answer 9. personal answer. 10. personal answer.

How to Become a Christian

Everyone in the theater was sitting on the edge of the seat. The helpless victim was being swept uncontrollably down the flooded stream. A willing helper waited downstream on the bank. Extending his arm, he screamed to the victim to grab and hold on. The rescuer wanted to save the victim, but the flooded stream was carrying the helpless person closer to death.

The Bible presents a similar picture. Each person can put himself or herself in place of the victim portrayed in the film. But our situation is real and has eternal consequences. The Bible says that all people have sinned. This means that we have turned against God by failing to put Him first in our lives. We all must be rescued from the consequences of sin. The Bible says, "The wages of sin is death; but the gift of God is eternal life through Jesus Christ our Lord" (Romans 6:23). Jesus is the eternal Rescuer, reaching out and pleading that we come to Him in faith. Jesus died on a cross to pay the penalty of sin, paying a price that we could not pay for ourselves. When we place our faith in Him, Jesus can rescue us from the certain penalty of sin. The Bible calls the penalty for sin eternal punishment in a literal place called hell. Only Jesus can rescue us from hell.

You have a choice to make. The Bible says that, "If thou shalt confess with thy mouth the Lord Jesus, and shalt believe in thine heart that God hath raised him from the dead, thou shalt be saved" (Romans 10:9).

Will you place your faith in Jesus right now? If you are ready to trust Christ as your Savior and Lord, invite Christ into your heart right now. Tell God in prayer that you know you are a sinner, that you want to repent of your sin, and then ask Him to forgive you. "Whosoever shall call on the name of the Lord shall be saved" (Acts 2:21).Then make public your confession of faith this Sunday in a church worship service.

The Church Study Course

The Church Study Course is a Southern Baptist educational system consisting of short courses for adults and youth combined with a credit and recognition system. More than 500 courses are available in 23 subject areas. Credit is awarded for each course completed. These credits may be applied to one or more of the 100 plus diploma plans in the recognition system. Diplomas are available for most leadership positions as well as general diplomas for all Christians. These diplomas are the certification that a person has completed from 5 to 8 prescribed courses. Diploma requirements are given in the catalogs.

Complete details about the Church Study Course system, courses available, and diplomas offered may be found in a current copy of the *Church Study Course Catalog* and in the study course section of the *Church Materials Catalog.* Study course materials are available from Baptist Book Stores.

The Church Study Course system is sponsored by the Sunday School Board, Woman's Missionary Union, and Brotherhood Commission of the Southern Baptist Convention.

How to Request Credit for This Course

This book is the text for course number 04-169 in the subject area: "BIBLE STUDIES." This course is designed for 5 hours of group study.

Credit for this course may be obtained in two ways:

1. Read the book and attend class sessions. (If you are absent from one or more sessions, complete the "Personal Learning Activities" for the material missed.)
2. Read the book and complete the "Personal Learning Activities." (Written work should be submitted to an appropriate church leader.)

A request for credit may be made on Form 725 "Church Study Course Enrollment/Credit Request" and sent to the Awards Office, Sunday School Board, 127 Ninth Avenue, North, Nashville, Tennessee 37234. The form on the following page may be used to request credit.

A record of your awards will be maintained by the Awards Office. Twice each year copies will be sent to churches for distribution to members.

CHURCH STUDY COURSE ENROLLMENT/CREDIT REQUEST

FORM - 725 (Rev. 1-89)

MAIL THIS REQUEST TO

CHURCH STUDY COURSE AWARDS OFFICE
BAPTIST SUNDAY SCHOOL BOARD
127 NINTH AVENUE, NORTH
NASHVILLE, TENNESSEE 37234

Is this the first course taken since 1983? ☐ **YES** If yes, or not sure complete all of Section 1. ☐ **NO** If no, complete only bold boxes in Section 1.

SECTION 1 - STUDENT I.D.

Social Security Number

Personal CSC Number*

STUDENT

☐ Mr. ☐ Miss
☐ Mrs. ☐

DATE OF BIRTH — Month / Day / Year

Name (First, MI, Last)

Street, Route, or P.O. Box

City, State — Zip Code

CHURCH

Church Name

Mailing Address

City, State — Zip Code

SECTION 2 - CHANGE REQUEST ONLY (Current inf. in Section1)

☐ Former Name

☐ Former Address — Zip Code

☐ Former Church — Zip Code

SECTION 3 - COURSE CREDIT REQUEST

	Course No.	Title (use exact title)
1.	04-169	Hosea: God's Redeeming Love
2.		
3.		
4.		
5.		
6.		

SECTION 4 - DIPLOMA ENROLLMENT

Enter exact diploma title from current Church Study Course catalog. Indicate diploma age group if appropriate. Do not enroll again with each course. When all requirements have been met, the diploma will be mailed to your church. Enrollment in Christian Development Diplomas is automatic. No charge will be made for enrollment or diplomas.

Title of Diploma — Age group or area

Title of Diploma — Age group or area

Signature of Pastor, Teacher, or Other Church Leader — Date

*CSC # not required for new students. Others please give CSC # when using SS # for the first time. Then, only one ID # is required.